Philippe Bauduin

SECOND WORLD WAR
INVENTIONS

OREP
EDITIONS

CONTENTS

FOREWORD

The great 'disasters' of the early 20th century

Three notable events early in the 20th century mobilised the inventive genius of mankind:
- The sinking of the Titanic, which directly affected the discovery of sonar then radar.
- The Great War during which great progress was made in caring for the wounded and, more particularly, in aviation.
- The widespread epidemic of Spanish Flu in the winter of 1918-1919 which – claiming more victims than the war itself – led to the later discovery of penicillin and antibiotics. So, it was in the thirties that numerous commodities, appliances and devices taken for granted today were discovered: antibiotics, sulphonamides, radar, turbojets, synthetic rubber, mineral oils, radiotelephony, and artificial intelligence... but it was only the outbreak of the Second World War that gave rise to their development and industrial use.

The Second World War and the Battle of Normandy

In four years of war, nowhere did the belligerents use rival technological advances more than in Normandy. Three million soldiers armed with the very latest devices: hundreds of sets of radar and as many V1 ramps and V2 launchers, the first jet aircraft, portable telephones, computers, hitherto unknown logistics applied to both blood and water, dozens of landing strips, thousands of nylon parachutes and incredible prefabricated ports (of which Arromanches still boasts imposing vestiges), confronted the bemused and horrified eyes of the people of Normandy. In the summer of 1944, superimposed on a Normandy in ruins, there was a Detroit of vehicles in assembly lines under the apple trees, and an emirate of pipelines. In addition to which military hospitals housed 40,000 beds where the wounded benefited from the most advanced treatment, such as the celebrated antibiotic, penicillin. As Hippocrates said long ago, 'If you aspire to be a surgeon, join the army and follow it everywhere.'

With the exception of atomic weaponry, Normandy became the theatre of confrontation of all these technological advances.
The pages that follow offer an account of 50 discoveries chosen at will among many others, that, in giving the reader a wider understanding of technological advances, sheds new light on the scale of Operation Overlord. Thus, visitors to the Landing Beaches can appreciate how humanity as a whole has profited from all the inventions collated during the Battle of Normandy.

Every cloud has a silver lining.

Ersatz - to replace the real thing

Hitler may have said to Mussolini, 'I will teach you how to make butter from coal, when you teach me how to make pullovers from macaroni.' This is a witticism, given that American chemists were, at the time, already producing woollen yarn from soybeans.

Whilst the main force of industrial and agricultural production was directed towards military use, it appeared clear that, as with rubber and petrol, there was a need for a synthetic counterpart for every other product.

When necessity is of the essence, the genius of man has no limits. In the Imhausen factories in Witten, Ruhr, German chemists therefore succeeded in producing

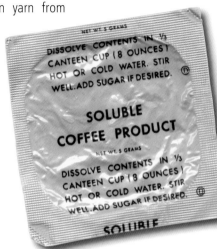

American 'K-rations' including corn and soybean extracts with added synthetic vitamins.

synthetic fat from coal to a ratio of 70 tonnes of coal for one tonne of nutrient. Production rose to 2,000 tonnes a year. This ersatz butter was so delicious that it was reserved for the regime's most favoured recruits: the submariners. Sugar was produced from wood in the form of a by-product – 'turfural', which was not only used to produce synthetic mineral oil and rubber, but also for compounds such as nylon.

Sugar could also be used to make yeasts that, in turn, offered potential for a range of other products. Milei, a German firm, invented an egg substitute from a milk and skimmed-milk base. All these ersatz products: sugars, fats, alcohols, yeasts, soaps, etc. were exported to all the occupied countries of Europe, in exchange for more noble products, which were immediately deployed to serve the German war effort.

Meanwhile, the Allies were far from idle, as we have seen regarding mineral oils and rubber; however, it was in the field of foodstuffs that the most remarkable progress was made. The approach was different: the famous K-ration for GIs, comprised soybean-based biscuits, designed to replace corned beef. In the event of a water shortage in Normandy, soap that could lather in sea water was also produced.

Whilst synthetic substitutes gained renown during the Second World War, the USA also offered a brand new prospect by developing vegetables that grew without soil to feed their troops. Tomatoes and lettuce were grown on gravel in a solution of nutrients and selective weedkiller, under arc-lamps. This was referred to as hydroponic cultivation.

These two developments: synthetics and hydroponics – were considerably improved later.

FOOD

Hybrid Maize

Maize is a cereal native to the North American Continent that can be traced back to prehistoric times in Mexico and New Mexico. Christopher Columbus brought the grain back to Spain on returning from his first expedition in 1483.

Back in the thirties, the Americans created a hybrid and entirely artificial form of maize, via cross fertilisation. The result was intended to highlight the desirable qualities of the strains involved. The disadvantage, however, was that these qualities were not passed on and fresh seeds needed to be produced for each crop sown. Following their entry into the war, in order to increase their beef, poultry and milk yield – but also to augment the latent potential in maize, plastics and synthetic rubber elements – the USA embarked extensively on the culture of hybrid products. By 1945, records showed that up to 100 'quintaux' (hundredweight) per hectare had been harvested in Indiana and in Iowa, where agriculture had become 100% hybrid. Production had risen from an average of 14 quintaux in the thirties to 35 quintaux in 1942 to 1945.

Shortly after the Liberation, a misunderstanding of the subtleties of Uncle Sam's language led the French to eat yellow bread instead of grey bread, by ordering corn flour rather than wheat flour. Under the Marshall Plan, France was to import 30 tonnes of hybrid seed-corn that would produce up to 52 quintaux to the hectare instead of 10 quintaux. The usefulness of hybrid maize had been fully demonstrated. In 1950, 1,000 tonnes of seed were imported. Following an agreement between the USA and France, the INRA produced French hybrids that are now in current use. The result was a ten-fold increase in production.

Nescafé-Nestea

Coffee was first consumed around the year 850 in Abyssinia. A goatherd by the name of Kaldi was surprised to find his goats particularly spirited after eating certain red berries. Testing them himself, he noted their stimulating effect. His fellow countrymen, noting the effect it produced, then began to cultivate coffee. Although perhaps mere legend, the story is nevertheless worth telling. Coffee was first exported from Yemen to conquer Europe via Constantinople and the Austro-Hungarian Empire.

France promoted its cultivation in its colonies, particularly in the West Indies, from where it spread to Brazil.

In the thirties, Brazil overproduced coffee to such an extent that it was burned in railway engines, and Nestlé was asked to use a share of the excess crop in order to resume its research to produce a soluble coffee which, to date, had not proved satisfactory.

First attempts failed to retain the coffee's full-bodied aroma. In 1937, by adding carbohydrates, naturally present in coffee, Nestlé obtained a soluble powder that was named Nescafé and duly patented. In 1938, Nestlé similarly produced tea under the brand name Nestea.

1938 and 1939 sales results were disappointing. The first major order came from the American Army, and where commercial advertising had failed, the GIs succeeded worldwide, offering an introduction beyond the firm's dreams. The magic powder arrived on the Normandy beaches, where you can still find examples from the same period, with no shelf-life indicated, but with their original coffee aroma intact. In May 1945, when the American troops met the Russians, the former offered packets of Nescafé to the latter, who, oblivious to its properties, consumed it undiluted. It is said that the effect on the Russians was similar to that of Kaldi the goatherd, and, in some cases, soldiers suffered heart attacks.

FOOD

Soybean

Soybean is a leguminous plant known to the Chinese since over 4,000 years. It was introduced to the USA at the very beginning of the 20th century, when its cultivation spread rapidly. First statistics appeared in 1924 with a production of 135,000 tonnes.

Upon their entry into the war, U.S. Army production topped 5 million tonnes of soybean and its use as food for both humans and animals, together

Synthetic wool made from soybean could be used to produce particularly sturdy fabric for clothing. It was also used to make hats, upholstery fabric and even mats.

with other applications, was already commonplace. Concurrently, the exploitation of its pharmaceutical properties also advanced.

Richer in calories and proteins than beef, it was claimed that 500 grammes of soya flour contained as much protein as a kilogramme of beef. With vitamins A, B1, C, G and K all present in soybean, we can understand why the U.S. Army included soybean biscuits in their famous 'K' Rations, largely consumed throughout Normandy at the time of the Liberation. Elsewhere, a number of food substitutes such as oil and fat were also made from soybean, which replaced peanut oil

in American margarine. The most remarkable achievements, however, concerned its industrial use. Soybean-based plastics were used for the construction of cars and aircraft. It appears that both the steering wheel and the distributor head of the Jeep were cast in a plastic extract made using soybean. Yarn similar to wool could also be spun into very supple thread. Many other applications are worthy of mention: insecticides, inks, rubbers, etc.

In addition, the residue obtained after the extraction of oil formed a by-product, which proved so useful and inexpensive in feeding cattle and poultry cost that it soon became the main food base in use in Europe.

A Jeep steering wheel with a plastic distributor head made using soybean.

Synthetic wool made using soybean.

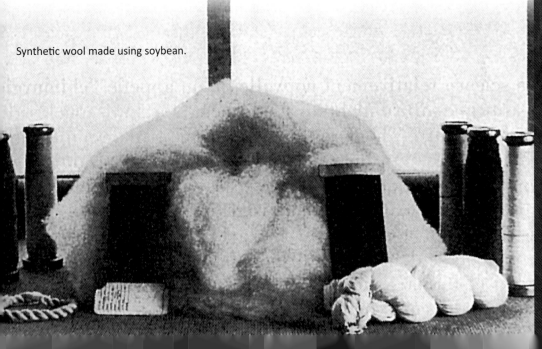

Glued, laminated and impregnated wood

Whilst one of the first composite developments was unquestionably plywood, laminated and glued wood is also worthy of note. The process involves cutting thin sheets of wood which are glued together with the grain of each sheet at different angles to avoid warping. This process was essentially used in aircraft production. Whereas, in the thirties, aircraft construction using metal was deemed a major breakthrough, the

De Havilland Mosquito 'The Wooden Wonder'.

rarity and cost of metal in times of war, led to the return of wood, and the development of a laminated product. Impregnated with synthetic resin, which eliminated empty spaces, it offered a material that was both organically and water resistant. Progress in the use of wood served for aircraft tail pieces and for the entire fuselage of the twin-engine de Havilland Mosquito consisting of layers of glued and laminated hardwood and balsa. This brings to mind the impressive feat by RAF Group Captain Pickard and Colonel Livry-Level's Mosquitoes, who, on the 18th of February 1944, brought down the perimeter walls of the prison in Amiens to liberate 258 prisoners condemned to death by the Gestapo – an operation fittingly codenamed 'Jericho'.

Wood, when de-grained, impregnated and compressed, is transformed into a new material that can be used to produce mechanical parts, such as gears, together with electronic and electromechanical components. Today, not only do we find it in magnificent timber structures, but also in interior motor vehicle fittings, and even in their construction. Its lightweight and corrosion-free qualities, together with its capacity for simple recycling, render it a highly attractive material.

The Wooden Wonder Spitfire propellers in impregnated wood.

Synthetic rubber

In 1880, G. Bouchardat prepared synthetic rubber using isoprene which he had extracted from natural rubber! Four years later, rubber was produced from isoprene, this time extracted from turpentine. One may well wonder what use could be made of synthetic rubber produced from real rubber.

In the early 20th century, a number of establishments invested in projects aimed at perfecting the production of rubber made from hydrocarbons.

I.G. Farben, in Germany, produced Buna, invented by Bock via a butadiene (also a C4H6 hydrocarbon) reaction with sodium, hence obtaining synthetic rubber offering superior quality to that of natural rubber. In 1839, Charles Goodyear, founder of the Goodyear Company, invented the vulcanisation process (the processing of rubber with sulphur compounds to improve its strength). The company acquired the British patents in 1927

LONDON NEWS   JULY 22, 1944

HOW DID THE TREE GET INTO THE BOTTLE?

Recently, because of the war emergency, the words "synthetic rubber" have come before the public eye. Yet in actual fact, the first substance resembling the natural rubber that grows in the rubber tree, the first synthetic (or substitute) rubber to come out of the Goodyear laboratories, was produced as long as 17 years ago. And the same painstaking and unwavering application to research which evolved the first cube of synthetic rubber, and which indeed constitutes the very life-blood of progress itself, is to be found to-day—as it is always—inside the Goodyear research laboratories.

In the new world that we are all to-day fighting to win—and for which Goodyear is everywhere battling in the front line— Goodyear will continue to play its part. That part, if the Goodyear research scientists have their say, will be the building of a life which will be easier and happier for more and more people.

Another

GOODYEAR

contribution to Progress

and produced its first synthetic rubber (S.B.R. – Styrene Butadiene Rubber) tyres. Then, in 1930, two Americans – J.A. Nieuland and W.H. Carothers – discovered Neoprene: an oil-resistant and heat-resistant synthetic rubber made by polymerising chloroprene. After Pearl Harbor, the rubber plantations in the Far East were under Japanese occupation. America, the most motorised country in the world, applied rationing and restricted motor transport in order to limit the use of tyres. Research for rubber from petrochemicals or from butadiene originating from grain alcohol. In 1942, the United States formed a pool of private companies, referred to as the G.R.S. – Government Rubber System, which was placed under Federal control. Deprived of hevea rubber from the Far East, due to the Allied naval blockade, the Germans took similar action.

In Normandy, Allied and German transport alike were equipped with synthetic rubber tyres. Today, all tyre manufacturers use synthetic rubber which accounts for over 80% of the total rubber content used in tyres.

If, today, we were to reflect on the great scientists or inventors that marked the creative spirit of the 20th century, those that come to mind may include: Fleming, Turing, Grignard, etc. however, few would probably mention Fischer and Tropsch.

Yet, in 1923, Franz Fischer and Hans Tropsch, both researchers at the Kaiser-Wilhelm-Institute für Kohlenforschung, discovered how to produce synthetic hydrocarbon from coal gas, hence marking a genuine revolution in the production of motor fuels into the 21st century. For the first time ever, Fischer and Tropsch successfully transformed gas into liquid.

To obtain a hydrocarbon, we must bring H2 into contact with CO. CO forms when either carbon or natural gas is brought into contact with oxygen.

The H2-CO compound is passed through a catalyst to become a liquid hydrocarbon. The fact that catalysts could produce a chemical modification without the elements being consumed had been established at BASF since 1910.

The first industrial plant to produce synthetic motor oil was set up in Germany in 1935. During the war, 9 factories were opened, collectively capable of producing 16,000 barrels of synthetic motor fuel per day, total German production in 1944 being estimated at 4.5 million barrels. Cobalt was first used as a catalyst; however, when it became scarce, it was replaced with iron. As mentioned elsewhere, it was by perfecting their logistics that the Allies were assured victory, but also by destroying that of their adversaries. This was patently so regarding enemy oil production.

After the war, two synthetic oil plants were dismantled and set up in the USA as models to test their performance.

Similarly, in South Africa during the sanctions against apartheid, two plants were set up using large coal deposits from open-cast mines.

Today, with the increasing price of the barrel, this technology has become highly competitive. The need to drill for oil at great depths increases production costs. Reserves are limited, whilst resources of gas and coal are huge. On this basis, the production of synthetic oil can be perfectly envisaged near coal fields and sources of natural gas.

Nylon

In 1922, the German chemist and Nobel prize-winner, Hermann Standniger (1959), discovered the principle of polymerisation, namely a large molecule formed from repeated units of smaller molecules and known as a macromolecule.

In 1928, the Du Pont de Nemours Company, founded in the USA in 1802 by an immigrant French chemist to make gunpowder, decided to diversify and engaged a research team among whom the brilliant Harvard graduate chemist Wallace H. Carothers. In 1930, when allowing mixed molecules to heat for longer than intended, W.H. Carothers discovered — by pure chance — a new polyamide from which threads could be made. After further and lengthy research, it became nylon, which was patented in 1937.

Due to its fine and light texture, it was immediately used for ladies' stockings. As from its entry into the war, the U.S. Army, perfectly aware of its qualities, requisitioned total production for military use. And since nylon is stronger and lighter than silk, it was used to make parachutes from the very start.

H. Standinger.

These were first used in the Pacific, at Midway, in 1942. At dawn on the 6th June 1944, thousands of Allied paratroops, using nylon parachutes, descended from the skies of Normandy to secure

the flanks of the landing bridgeheads: the Americans at the base of the Cotentin peninsula and the British in the Orne Bay.

A few days only sufficed for the girls in Normandy to make blouses and skirts from this new, light and stylish material, in a range of colours. Indeed, the parachutes had been dyed in different colours to denote their various uses.

It is rather difficult today for us to imagine life without nylon.

CHEMICAL ENGINEERING

Reinforced plastics

If plastics in general are acknowledged as a major development between the two wars, notably in aviation, their use with fibres has also produced new materials, known as composites. Composite materials are produced by a process that exists in the natural environment. They are formed by associating a matrix with fibres, the fibres bringing qualities that are not possessed by the matrix. A good example of this is that of wood fibres immersed in lignin.

Fibre materials were developed from the very onset of the war. They were mainly forms of fibreglass invented by a Frenchman by the name of Du Bonnel. Glass fibres were coated with a matrix of polyesters, whilst wood fibres were impregnated with synthetic resin.

The qualities of fibreglass: its light weight, resistance to humidity, its strength allied with performance in varying temperatures, make it ideal for the production of reinforced plastics, using either long or short fibres.

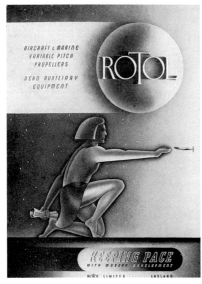

Rotol: the first British company to produce propellers in reinforced plastic.

In the USA, Britain and Germany, reinforced plastics were employed in the production of components that were lightweight and boasted greater shock resistance and toughness than metal. In addition, they were less costly and quicker to produce.

In view of these qualities, reinforced plastics were first used in the aeronautical and electronics fields: aircraft tail panels, fuel tanks, propellers and aerials, etc.

More recently in the United Kingdom, over and above the usual fibreglass, long optical fibres have been used in composite materials, through which a laser beam is passed, highlighting constraints. Hence, the first intelligent composites were born!

Silicones

At the end of the 19th century, a number of eminent scholars were already conducting research on silicium. Among them, the British scientist Kipping hit on what was to become 'silicones'.

The mathematician Victor Grignard, born in Cherbourg in 1871, who was also working on silicium in Lyon, discovered the famous test that was named after him. It was a radical development which earned him the Nobel Prize in Chemistry in 1912. As a professor based in Besançon, Grignard may well have forgotten his native Normandy. The Great War, however, brought him back to Cherbourg when he was called up and found himself in the highly strategic post of guarding a level-crossing!

V. Grignard.

Grignard's discoveries led Kipping to devise a whole family of silicones in the 1920s, together with their many potential applications. Their practical use did not come until the beginning of the Second World War, when two great American industrial groups: Dow Corning and General Electric, realised their great potential.

Their prodigious properties for insulation and as a moisture repellent formed the basis of their most notable military uses: the protection of spark plugs in aircraft at high altitudes, the encapsulation of electronic equipment such as radar, for use as a demoulding agent when turning out casts both in the rubber industry and for foodstuffs. Other uses, where information as to their use was at the time under wraps, included silicone oils in aircraft shock absorbers, involving a

specific property produced by the action of molecules sliding against each other, and which enhanced the absorbers' mechanical effect.

The war period saw considerable development in the use of silicones, notably thanks to the German scientist Müller and the American Rochow.

The annual production of silicones now exceeds a million tonnes, with such a diversity of uses that it is impossible to list them all. The biocompatibility of silicones renders them particularly useful in the production of implants and surgical accessories, kitchen utensils and for silicone-based anti-adhesives, or for waterproofing fabrics.

Enigma & the computers

Cryptoanalysis, or how to decipher secret enemy messages, has existed for over two-thousand years. In 40 BC, the Spartans used the 'Scytale': a baton with a thin strip of parchment, bearing a message. When removed from the baton, the contents of the scroll were indecipherable by the messenger taking them to the recipient. The latter, however, had an identical baton which, once covered with the parchment, revealed the secret message.

In 1934, Hitler had a coding machine made to code on an entirely new principle, considered to be indecipherable: the Enigma coder, the 20th century version of the Scytale. It was actually a copy of a commercial machine invented by a Dutchman, Hugo Koch, who had already patented it in 1919, before conceding his invention to a German who renamed it Enigma. Although it met with no commercial success, applied in military settings, it was a supposedly unbreakable code. Having acquired a commercial version of Enigma, the Polish secret services employed mathematicians to devise an analytical decoding method. Concurrently, in 1937, their French counterparts, under Colonel Gustave Bertrand, brought pressure to bear on a German who 'revealed' the secret of Enigma, in exchange for cash. Whenceforth, France could decode all German messages.

Finally, in June 1938, a Polish Jew known by the name of Lewinski, who had worked with the Germans on the Enigma code machine, informed MI 6 that he had obtained all the secrets of Enigma from a replica he had made himself. MI 6 sent an expert in coding and a young mathematician, Alan Turing, to Warsaw to take note of what they had learned from Lewinski. This being done, the British Government decided in 1938 to construct an automatic decoding machine following Turing's conclusions; the machine came to be known as 'The Bomb'. Although far from what we now know as a modern computer, it did bear certain similarities. Hence, on the 9th of January 1939, the Poles, the French and the British, all of whom were familiar with the Enigma code, held a meeting at the Château de Bois-Vignolles in France to

Enigma : millions of combinations to encode a three-letter word.

COMMUNICATION

coordinate their efforts and send their deciphering specialists with their equipment to Bletchley Park (north of London) to avoid them falling into enemy hands. At this point in time, France had already decoded 141 messages and allowed the British – thanks to 'The Bomb' – to decode a further 15,000. Yet, as strange as it may seem, Poland, France and Britain – all now perfectly aware of Hitler's plans – were nevertheless taken by surprise. This is, without all doubt, the greatest enigma of the war.

The Battle of Britain was waged in July, August and September 1940. Although it is acknowledged that the valorous RAF pilots and radars were largely to thank for the victory over the *Luftwaffe*, we tend to forget that Britain deciphered all orders emitted via Enigma, which – of course – in no way belittles the courage of the former.

Since the battle had met with failure, the Germans then set to bombarding British towns.

On the 14th of November 1940, a decoded Enigma message revealed the impending bombardment of Coventry. Duly informed, Churchill had to decide whether to evacuate the city, revealing to the Germans that the code had been broken, or to allow them to carry out the raid… He opted for the latter.

As the number of messages to decipher grew to around 10,000 a day, Flowers and Chandler were given the task of devising a more powerful decoder: Colossus. It was the result of work published in an article by Turing on the 26th of May 1936 in which he described an unprecedented, automated, rational, abstract, all-embracing machine, capable of programming other

Alan Turing (1912-1954).

machines, endowed with instructions and data that appeared on tape, and where the machine would record its results before automatically stopping. At the same time, Turing, a pupil of Einstein at Princeton, worked in collaboration with von Neumann and, whilst it will never be known what influence one had on the other, Turing is unquestionably the father of the computer and of artificial intelligence. Throughout the war, Turing and Neumann met in secret.

Chandler and Flowers believed that, concurrent to Colossus, Turing had produced an electronic and electromechanical computer. On the night of the 25th to the 26th of June 1944, the Germans sent a message coded by Enigma, informing that an armoured column was advancing towards Pegasus Bridge. They were unaware that this was an Allied acoustic lure. On the evening of the 2nd of August, an Enigma message from Juvincourt described E. Sommer's reconnaissance in his jet plane over Normandy, indicating all the Allied positions. One could continue over endless examples of German coded messages, which were immediately deciphered by the Allies.

When the war ended, in order to ensure that the reason for the Allied success was kept secret, Churchill ordered for the destruction of Colossus and all similar apparatus. In doing so, he thus destroyed considerable technical prowess which could have been transferred for industrial use. In compensation for this offence to the History of science, Colossus was reconstructed in 1999; sadly, this did not bring Turing back to life, for, whilst their machines were destroyed, most of those who had used them 'disappeared' mysteriously. Turing, allegedly unbalanced, was convicted for homosexuality and 'committed suicide' on the 7th of June 1954.

Turing's genius is now internationally acknowledged.

The Colossus computer. Note the paper tapes with transmission by perforation.

Permanent magnets

Lodestone, a natural form of magnetite has been known since Antiquity as an artificial magnet. In 1600, William Gilbert tried to make artificial magnets using field polar magnetism. The discovery by Oersted in 1820 of the magnetic field created by an electric current put a brake on attempts to produce artificial magnets. Not until 1931 did the Japanese Mishina discover an alloy of iron, nickel and aluminium, that had the exciting properties of a permanent magnet. It was named: 'Alnico'.

In 1938, Olivier and Shedden, in the course of the cooling process applied a magnetic field to the alloy and obtained some remarkable performances.

Alnico was found to have excellent magnetic properties and great durability that made it an essential component for all military systems developed during the Second World War by all the belligerents.

Artificial magnets can now be found in every branch of industry:
- electronic/electro-acoustic, radar, loud-speakers, microphones, gyroscopes, telephones, teleprinters, tape recorders...
- electrotechnology, generators, magnetos, and magnet motors, relays, switches, contact-makers, butterfly valves...
- measurement instruments: ammeters, voltmeters, electric comptometers or speedometers, clocks...

Thanks to work by Louis Néel from 1944-1946, it became possible to make artificial magnets using metallic powders which proved a simpler method. L. Néel was awarded the Nobel Prize in 1970.

An advertisement by Philips for Ticonal magnets.

The handie-talkie

The Dane V. Poulsen and an American R.A. Fessenden invented the forerunner to the radiotelephone in 1902. In 1940, Motorola examined the question of producing a portable radio telephone, in the form of a two-way transmitter-receiver, i.e. enabling to speak and listen simultaneously with a given frequency modulation: the Handie Talkie. The first completed system was used by the Bowling Green Police, Kentucky, in 1941.

Designed to be carried in one hand, the Army Handbook stated that it should not weigh more than 5 lbs and have a range of between 1.6 and 4.8 kilometres. The Handie Talkie worked on a band of frequencies between 3.5 and 6 MHz.

One of the frequencies mentioned was crystal controlled. Within a very small space, a little larger than a telephone, 30 x 8.5 x 8 cm2, it contained 5 vacuum tubes; transistors were only invented in 1948. It was a perfect pearl of miniaturisation. The tubes required a high-tension 103.5 volt battery and the filaments needed a 1.5v battery. The batteries alone weighed 900 grammes, i.e. almost eight times the weight of a modern mobile phone.

Handie-Talkie signals the **attack!**

HANDIE-TALKIE IS ANOTHER MOTOROLA RADIO FIRST!

If there is glory at all in war, *all of it goes without question to the men who do the fighting*. We who are on the production front turn out the weapons for Victory and simple satisfaction in the knowledge that our product *delivers* when needed.

The Handie-Talkie is a battery powered radio receiver and transmitter no larger than a cracker box. The operator talks, giving information, and listens, receiving instructions. Officers and men call it the "lightingest" radio in the army! The "Handie-Talkie" was developed by Motorola Electronics Engineers working closely with the U. S. Army Signal Corps. It is a Motorola *built* to be first!

Motorola Engineers who were famous in peacetime for radio that delivered peak performance will write pleasant surprises for you in Motorola Post-War Radios for Home and Car.

GALVIN MFG. CORPORATION • CHICAGO 51

Motorola Radio

F M RADIO • PHONOGRAPHS • RADAR • TELEVISION • POLICE RADIO • MILITARY RADIO COMMUNICATIONS

LIGHTER MOMENTS with **fresh** Eveready Batteries

"Is that you, darling? — I mean, there is no activity to report, Sergeant!"

"EVEREADY" "MINI-MAX" batteries power walkie-talkies (portable 2-way radios), as well as other communications equipment. Because our entire production goes to the armed forces your dealer may not be able to supply you till after the war.

The words "Eveready" and "Mini-Max" are trade-marks of National Carbon Co., Inc.

Buy War Bonds—as many as you can so often or you can!

MINI-MAX V BATTERY PORTABLE RADIO

EVEREADY

60

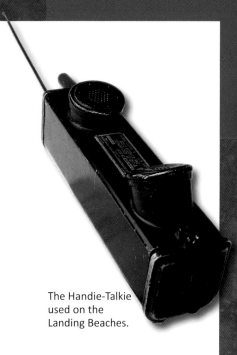

The Handie-Talkie used on the Landing Beaches.

The 'Iridium' portable telephone.

All the American units landing on D-Day were equipped with the Handie Talkie. Even today, it is not unusual to find one in working order, if you are lucky enough to find the right batteries. This forerunner of the mobile telephone disappeared with the arrival of transistors. The expertise acquired by Motorola provided a forward leap. Another notable advance by this company – the transponder, provided Neil Armstrong with a relay from the Moon to Earth in 1969. 'A small step...'

It was also Motorola that won the 'Always further, always smaller' race, in producing the first portable satellite telephone capable of communicating with all areas of the world: the Iridium system. A constellation of 66 satellites in low orbit, launched into space by the rockets Delta, Long March or Proton, connected a network of 11 stations on Earth making telephone communication possible from whatever position on land, sea or in space. It may be noted in passing that 66 plus 11 makes 77, corresponding exactly to the number of electrons gravitating around the nucleus of Iridium.

Motorola was quick to meet with rivals – from the early 20th century, Global Star (Loral-France Telecom), Skybridge (Alcatel) and Teledesic (Microsoft) were to prove ambitions competitors.

COMMUNICATION

Military deception

In January 1941, to demoralise the Italian garrison besieged in Bardia in Libya, the British Army used a gramophone and loudspeakers to simulate tank movements through the night, inciting the Italians to surrender at first light. This concept of psychological warfare was developed within the framework of Overlord, notably by the Royal Engineers who specialised in producing items of military deception. They were based at Colombiers-sur-Seulles in Calvados. The 'Deception Unit' made fake tanks and fake planes on fake airstrips... to deceive the enemy. Vestiges of the war remain in Colombiers, yet it is the statue of Eros in Tierceville, the work of the architect and Parisian theatre scenographer, Major Papillon, who joined the British Army, that best marks the unit's time here.

Given the limitations of the Libyan experiment, the use of hi-fi cinema projectors was envisaged – like the ones developed by Metro-Goldwyn-Mayer in 1929, for open-air use in Hollywood. It is worthy of note that, in 1944, tape recorders only existed in Germany and magnetic sound was not used in USA cinemas. During the night of 25th to 26th June, the unit contrived to simulate the sound of a

Dummy with an explosive charge dropped by parachute in the Cotentin peninsula.

column of heavy armour by mounting two cinema projectors on a scout car with film soundtracks running at full blast, giving the impression of a tank column moving from Périers-sur-le-Dan and over Pegasus Bridge. A deciphered Enigma message proved the stratagem to be a complete success. It was consequently repeated with similar success in Fontenay-le-Penel, Rauray and Gouvix.

The quality of reproduction was not quite Imax stereo, but it did offer a new dimension to sound.

Inflatable Sherman carried by troops.

The tape recorder

In 1897, a Frenchman by the name of Janet described a possible method of sound reproduction by magnetising steel wire. In 1898, a Dane called Poulsen described and produced a 'Telegraphon', consisting of steel wire rolled round a cylinder, similar to the drums used in Edison's phonographs. The wire recorded magnetic signals from sounds through a microphone and played them back. Poulsen's invention was exhibited at the Universal Exhibition in Paris in 1900. Over the years, tape recorders on the steel-wire principle were updated. It was quite commonplace to find them in crashed aircraft of all nationalities in Normandy in 1944. On the German side, Pfleumeur patented his invention, consisting of a paper band with a thin coating of iron filings that retained magnetism.

In 1933, BASF expressed an interest in the latter and collaborated with AEG to produce magnetic heads consisting of an electro-magnet of which the air-gap was a fine slit causing the magnetic field to open out.

In 1935, BASF substituted powdered steel with a much finer magnetic film, produced by a chemical reaction.

AEG, BASF and Telefunken combined to produce the 'Magnetophon' as we now know it. The first concert recording was by the London Philharmonic Orchestra under the direction of Sir Thomas Beecham, given in BASF's own hall at Ludwigshafen on the 19th of November 1936. During the war, Germany mobilised a considerable amount of research et AEG Telefunken in the development of the tape recorder which proved to be a remarkable propaganda weapon in the hands of the Nazi regime. In 1941, the first professional tape recorder was exhibited at the Universum Berlin Film AG. The few copies on sale were immediately sold. The Allies noticed that Hitler's speeches and concerts were often broadcast by local radio stations which led them to believe that recordings were distributed throughout the country. The high quality of these transmissions met with worldwide astonishment. Among the most surprised there was a certain J. Mullin, on location in London as representative of a Californian cinema organisation. After the war, he managed to get hold of some tape recorders seized by the Allies and passed them on to Ampex who made copies. Hence, the era of tape recorders, cassette players, videoscopes and the like was born.

AEG tape recorder, 1936.

COMMUNICATION

Aerial photography

It is to Nadar, alias Felix Tourmachon, that we owe the first aerial photograph, taken aboard a balloon at an altitude of 520 metres, above Paris's Avenue du Bois de Boulogne, in 1858. Still under conservation at the CNAM, the picture features the Place de l'Etoile, clearly visible on the right. The same year, Nadar took out a patent for 'A new aerostatic photographic device'.

Whilst Wilbur Wright is credited with taking the first photograph from an aircraft, the exact date or place are unknown. It may have been either over Auvours near Le Mans in 1908, or Contocello in Italy in 1909.

The Great War certainly lent wings to the development of aerial photographic reconnaissance. It became possible to locate troop movements in the Battle of the Marne. Cameras and photographic material were constantly improved. Pictures once taken manually could later be taken by remote control. Photos could be taken, not only on planes and airships, but from balloons and even from kites.

Between the wars, the Allies abandoned their efforts at improving reconnaissance aircraft to concentrate on better maps and map-reading or geology. A few architects, such as Le Corbusier, used aerial photography for urban planning purposes. In the same period, the Germans used commercial aircraft to photograph their future prey: the USSR but also France and Britain.

The French and British, taken unawares, deployed ill-adapted reconnaissance aircraft, suffering heavy losses as a result. An Australian, S. Cotton, saved the situation by developing a new strategy. He used unarmed Spitfires, lighter, speedier and capable of flying at high altitude: 10,000 metres. The only means of defence available for these pilots was their consummate art of manoeuvre. S. Cotton suffered no losses.

The world's first aerial photograph, taken aboard an Ar34 jet plane, over Arro.

Whilst it was vital to locate enemy troop positions and defences in spite of camouflage and deceptive tactics, it was also necessary to discover military and industrial potential. Among the more outstanding photographs, we can note one by Flight Sergeant E. Peek. On the 23rd of June 1943, from his reconnaissance Mosquito, he took pictures of a V2 in take-off position on the firing-line at Peenemünde. In preparation for Overlord, millions of negatives were used, not only for map making but also to identify obstacles on the beaches, defences along the Atlantic Wall, etc. Around 26,000 negatives were produced daily, requiring some 60,000 prints. The demand was such that the British photographic industry soon ran short of the silver compound needed to make the emulsion. Supplies were sent by air from the USA. Use was made of both civil and military geographers and geologists to examine the photographs and to advise those involved in Military Intelligence. Among them, there was a certain Ian Fleming, who later 'invented' James Bond. Although it can be said that Lower Normandy was the most photographed location in the world, there were – despite all necessary care – a few omissions. For example, the hedges in the bocage came as an unpleasant surprise to the Allies.

In the hectic scramble to go faster and to attain greater heights, it was in fact the Germans who gained world admiration: with the first twinjet aircraft, the Arado 234. The plane's mission was to photograph targets for the V1 and V2 rockets and to correct the shots after first impact. The plane flew at a height of 12,000 metres and attained a speed of around 900 km/h. On the 2nd of August 1944, behind schedule due to Allied raids, though also due to action by the Resistance, the first Arado took off from Juvincourt in the Aisne area. Captain E. Sommer was on board. Unhindered, for an hour and a half, he flew over Normandy, three or four times, with a Zeiss RB 30/50 and a 50-302 millimetre focus high-performance camera. He took 380 remarkable photographs of the entire Allied logistics. The intelligence received and transmitted by Enigma from Juvincourt was to unleash the counter offensive from Mortain that same day, shortly before midnight.

Following the perfection of the Arado Jets came not only the U-2s but also the Drones, pilotless planes (self-propelled aircraft) that remained airborne, anything between a few minutes to several hours. There was also a kite with four cords that could carry cameras or even radar. The first negatives in space were taken in 1946 at an altitude of 130 km aboard a V2 rocket fired in the United States.

Today, satellites transmit digital pictures of the Earth for many uses: environmental, statistical, to identify planted and forest areas, flooded zones, for geological or archaeological research, etc.

The first satellite photo of the Earth dates back to 1959.

(See BAUDUIN P. et CHARON E., *Normandie 44. Les photos de l'avion espion*, Caen, 1997.)

Colour film and photography

The first colour photograph was obtained by a Frenchman, Gabriel Lippmann, in 1891, using interferential waves of light. He was awarded the Nobel Prize in 1908 and elected President of the Academy of Science in 1912. But it was only when the First World War struck that a genuine breakthrough was made in films. Two Americans, Leopold Godowsky and Leopold Mannes, perfected a duotone method for use in cinema films. In 1930, in collaboration with Kodak, they succeeded in producing a duotone film for use by amateur photographers. Five years later, they brought out a trichrome film, which was commercialised under the brand name Kodachrome.

G. Lippmann.

In 1928, another American, H. T. Kalmus, invented a new form: Technicolor.

In 1937, Agfa in Germany put Agfacolor on the market a few months ahead of Kodak's Ektakrome. All competitors were now lined up, and the race was on.

In 1939, a new Afgacolor negative-positive film was perfected. In America, the same year, MGM produced its famous record running-time film *Gone with the Wind*, directed by Victor Fleming.

In 1942, Kodak announced the launch of Kodacolor.

COMMUNICATION

Extracts from the original film taken aboard the B-17 Memphis Belle on its last raid on Wilhelmshaven in 1944.

In 1943, alter several abortive attempts, Germany produced, in Agfacolor, *The Adventures of Baron Munchausen*, a propaganda film, highlighting technical advances on the occasion of the 20th anniversary of the German film and TV company Universum Berlin Film AG. It was produced by J. von Báky. A few magazines at the time had begun to publish colour photographs: *Illustrated* in the UK and *Signal* in Germany. War

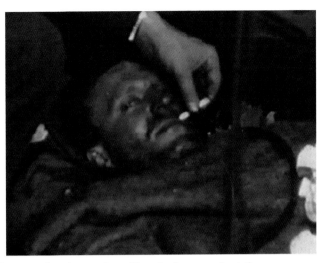

correspondents did not yet use colour. At the time, colour films in fact required three cameras combined: one for each primary colour. This did not make for easy transport.

Only two colour films in Kodachrome were produced for amateurs, for use on 16 mm cinema cameras. *Memphis* Belle merits a special mention. It was the true story of a B-17 based in England, filmed from inside the Bomber during a raid on Wilhemshaven. It depicts thrilling scenes of aerial dogfights. The series of films by George Stevens produced upon Eisenhower's permission are the only colour films on the Liberation of France. The striking images of the Landing Beaches, of Bernières, Caen, Saint Lô, Coutances, Carpiquet and Paris are worthy of note. These films, retrieved after their producer's death, were published by his son around twenty years ago.

Agfa's rights were dispersed after the war and were deployed to develop processes that are now in everyday use.

Radar

The history of Radar is a complicated one. In all nations, since Hertz's experiments in 1886, we now know that a radio-electric or optic wave reverberates against an obstacle and that the echo emitted can be recorded.

The sinking of the Titanic first incited research for devices to locate obstacles or objects in the sea.

In 1912, an Englishman invented a device to detect echoes in water: the sonar or echo-sounder – a genuine forerunner to radar.

During the thirties, thousands of others conducted research the world over, on angles or reflexion of sound waves on ships and aircraft. They worked on the basis of what later became radar. It is impossible to say who actually invented what is a collective work, but three names stand out: Sir Robert Watson-Watt of the N.P.L.,

Chain Home Radar on the east Coast of England in 1940.

Dr R. Kühnold and Maurice Ponte. Hence, in 1934, CSF applied for a patent for 'un nouveau système de repérage d'obstacles et ses applications – a new system of identifying obstructions and its fonctions. This device was used notably on a liner, the Normandie in 1936; not exactly in the form of radar as yet, but all the components were there.

By the end of the thirties, the British, the Germans and the French too, possessed a range of devices: extremely efficient ones, not merely to locate but to fire on targets.

Right from the beginning of the Second World War, the British erected large radar aerials: the Chain Home, to protect their coasts against attacks from German aircraft. It is now an acknowledged fact that RAF pilots and radar won the Battle of Britain.

On the 8th May of 1940, Maurice Ponte, an engineer with SFR – now THOMSON-CSF – brought his invention to the attention of the British: a transmitter valve – the 'magnetron' that proved to be a genuine breakthrough, and would later revolutionise the development of radar. In June 1940, on the Côte d'Azur, a French SFR radar detected a fleet of Italian bombers, enabling French fighters to partly destroy it.

Radar could henceforth become mobile, notably aboard aircraft. Philippe Livry-Level, a Flying Officer from Normandy who joined the RAF, tells how, thanks to radar, he managed to pursue enemy submarines in the Atlantic in 1942.

This brings us to Normandy, where the German occupants installed two radar surveillance networks: one naval and the other for aircraft. Some thirty aerials were set up along the Normandy coastline for both detection and as firing points. They were of four different types at the following sites: Dieppe, Fécamp, Cap-d'Antifer, Bruneval, Pourville, Les Andelys, Le Theil-Nolent, Houlgate, Douvres, Arromanches, Ducy-Sainte-Marguerite, Englesqueville, Saint-Pierre-Église, Clitourps, Cap-Lévy, Urville, Auderville-Hague, Jobourg, Beaumont-Hague, Sortosville, Saint-Pierre-la-Vieille, Vire...

SFR radar aboard the liner Normandie in 1936.

Six hours after the D-Day Landings, the first mobile radar was in use in the British Sector.

The British landed some 300 radar-equipped trucks in Normandy, and with at least equal numbers brought in by the Americans, we can safely say that the Normandy countryside was literally spiked with aerials.

Radar was in use just as much for navigation as for weather forecasting.

In the thirties, radio-navigation depended on land-based beacons, or on radio beacons like the one at Ver-sur-Mer that could provide an aircraft with its exact position. This was an elementary system of radio direction finding. Along with the three Allied systems used: Loran (USA) in hectometric waves, the British GEE in metric waves and DECCA (also British) but in kilometric waves, the German system, X-Gerät, radar was soon to be added.

During the landings, the Allies and the French Resistance used radar to guide inside gliders and to direct parachute landings. This was the 'Eureka-Rebecca' system mentioned by Livry-Level from 161 RAF Squadron in his secret missions. The landing-marker called Eureka was either dropped by parachute or put in place by men on the ground. It sent out a signal in reply to the one received by the Rebecca radar from the aircraft. The system was used by 300 planes on D-Day. The world over, researchers rivalled in ingenuity to develop various radar systems, both on the ground or aboard ships and aircraft, all of which were in use during the Battle of Normandy. The cost of research and development of the different types of radar was estimated at $2 billion, i.e. the equivalent of the German V1 and V2 rockets. After the war, many firms continued to develop radar. Among them, Raytheon, a company employing an engineer by the name of Percy Spencer. When studying the new magnetrons in 1946, Spencer noticed that the temperature of a snack placed near one of them had increased. Hence, the microwave oven was born.

German radar at Arromanches in 1944.

The magnetron was to bring good times to Normandy after the bad times. The wheel of fortune was turning.

COMMUNICATION

Industrial radiography

The German Wilhelm Conrad von Röntgen discovered X-Ray in 1895 in Würzburg. He was awarded the first Nobel Prize in Physics in 1901.

X-Ray was – for a long time – the only means of inspecting the human body, first of all the skeleton and later its organs. Medical generators used up to hundreds of kilovolts.

Use of radiography in industry was initially limited due to low voltage. It was only at the beginning of the war that G.E.C. managed to build a generator to provide a million volts, enabling internal pictures of large metal parts to be produced after they were manufactured.

W.C. Röntgen.

The device was adapted and rendered mobile under the impetus of the USAAF, to inspect damage to aircraft on their return from bombing raids. Inspection was carried out by X-Ray. Speedy identification of the damage meant quicker and more precise repairs.

The era of non-destructive verification – a precious tool for industry – was also born.

Non-destructive X-ray inspection of components.

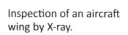

Inspection of an aircraft wing by X-ray.

'V-mail'

The 'Victory Post' was, with blood transfusion, a fine example of Allied organisation and logistics. Nothing was of greater importance to a soldier than prompt receipt of private mail – all the more so, since it implied that Supreme Command communications were finally in place. The psychological factor alone merited the efforts needed for an efficient armed forces postal service. The first Allied planes to land in France that were not directly concerned with military action were Hurricanes from the RAF 46th Group, specially assigned to transport mail. After the Battle of Britain, these aircraft were stripped of

Processing mail.

weaponry for lightness and speed; they landed at Saint-Croix-sur-Mer at 5.30am on Saturday 10th June. Reported so, this could appear to be a very commonplace event; however, it was in fact quite a feat. The Landings had begun only five days earlier, during which time the Engineers had constructed an air base so that those receiving their mail would know immediately that the military situation was stable. Speaking of Sainte-Croix, some noteworthy arrivals took place at this temporary airstrip under the command of J.E. Johnson. On the 13th of June, two FAFL

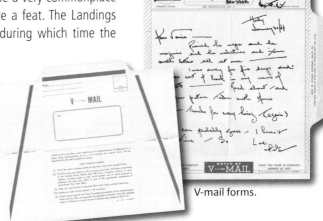

V-mail forms.

Squadrons of Spitfires belonging to the Free French Airforce landed. Among them, Denys Baudard grounded on French soil after a long period of exile. On the 15th of June, Eisenhower's B-17 touched down on this 1,200-metre runway. Last but not least, came the Fieseler-Storch on the 21st of June, aboard which... Winston Churchill.

Whilst the Hurricanes delivered British mail, they also brought messages for GIs, known as 'V-Mail' The messages to and from soldiers and their families were written on special forms. They were censored, coded, sorted and microfilmed, before being delivered to the troops. One case of microfilms replaced 37 sacks of mail.

COMMUNICATION

PLUTO

The degree of sophistication deployed during the Landings, in terms of military logistics: construction of ports, bridges, airfields and roads, placing of pipelines for oil or water, routing of vehicles etc. rivalled in quality with all the armed services, be they on sea, air or land.

Eisenhower, with pen to paper, asserted that, along with the prefabricated ports, the 'Pipeline under the Ocean' (PLUTO) was one of Overlord's two major innovations.

Connecting 6-inch pipelines.

During a demonstration in 1942 of a tank flame-thrower, fitted with a long flexible tube for fuel supply, Lord Louis Mountbatten asked the Minister for Fuel, Geoffrey Lloyd, if he would be able to

Floating cable drums (Conundrums) loaded with the pipeline that was laid across the Channel.

lay a flexible pipeline across the Channel between England and France. With existing experience in use of a flexible pipeline, aimed at setting the sea on fire to counter any possible attempt at invasion on the English coast, British firms set to developing PLUTO – among them, the British branch of the German firm Siemens, directed by Dr H.R. Wright.

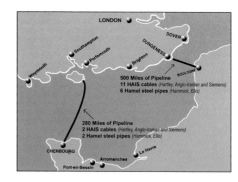

After several tests, they finally
adopted the technique of
a transatlantic telephone
cable. The idea was simply to
reproduce similar cable without
its copper core, hence leaving

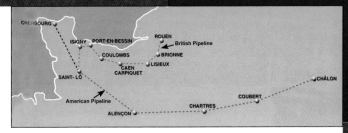

an empty tube for oil supply. The scheme proved less simple in practice; supple tubes were used
but they were made of steel.

Two lines were laid: one between the Isle of Wight and Cherbourg, comprising of two cables
and two pipes, for a total length of 280 miles. The other line between Dungeness and Boulogne
consisted of 11 cables and 6 pipes, for a total length of 500 miles. Pipeline links with Cherbourg
and Boulogne were made possible as the troops advanced. Meanwhile, the first cable was brought
ashore; it was then connected to the oil terminal, located in Port-en-Bessin.

Over and above the pipes and cables, the operation also required part cable-layer, part tanker
vessels. The cable drums, known as 'Conundrums', measuring 7 metres in diameter, 30 metres in
length and weighing in at 1,600 tonnes when fully loaded, were towed across the Channel by two
tugs. In addition, pumping stations were set up.

The first pipeline was in action by the 12th of June, in Port-en-Bessin: a provisional terminal in
advance of PLUTO. By the 24th of June, the first
pipelines came ashore on the sandy Beach of
Urville-Nacqueville, to the west of Cherbourg and,
on the 3rd of July, PLUTO became fully operational
and began to transport oil from England to
Normandy.

Non-stop round the clock, the system pumped
4 million litres of oil daily and, from the 12th of
August 1944 to the 8th of May 1945, 480 million.
Although the people of Normandy can recall
seeing pools of petrol in ditches alongside the
pipes, barely below ground level, leakage, in fact,
only amounted to 1.8%.

Astonishing technical success at the time, even if
pliable pipelines and off-shore platforms are now
in current use. Today, France is at the forefront
of these technologies and is a world-leader, with
– for example – an oil well at a depth of 1,709
metres, another record.

Pluto cable-layer aground on Urville-Nacqueville
Beach.

I t is to a certain John Dean of Whitstable in England that we owe the first breathing apparatus for use in adverse conditions.

In 1830, when his stable was in flames, John took the helmet from a suit of armour in his manor house and attached a tube through which his brother Charles pumped air from a winnower, thus managing to save his horses.

In 1832, he patented the device. In 1834 he adapted a helmet for diving in the Thames Estuary. In 1838, Augustus Siebe, an Australian, invented the first metal diving helmet fitted with a pump. He supplied the equipment to the French Navy.

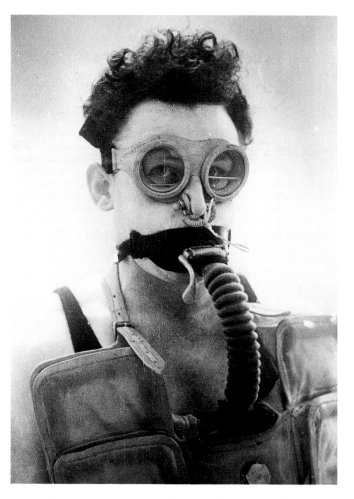

This type of equipment, Narguile, is totally dependent on the air supply from the surface and is consequently less mobile. In England, Henry Fleuss from the Siebe Gorman Company introduced a self-contained breathing apparatus with oxygen in 1870. Sir Robert Davis produced equipment to rescue submarine crews in danger, which was continually updated. Whilst gas emission presents no problem when working on submarines, this is generally not the rule for divers and swimmers on active service, where utmost discretion is the rule. The omission of bubbles or noise reveals their position.

Consequently, in 1942, German technicians from Siebe launched the first self-contained breathing apparatus capable of recycling exhaled gases, hence no bubbles and no sound – the 'Davis Submerged Escape Apparatus'. Toxic CO_2 was emitted into a compartment containing soda lime. Experiments with this diving gear cost the lives of many divers, due to physiological problems. It

OCEANOGRAPHY

could only be used to a depth of 7 metres. The divers and frogmen deployed to take samples of sand and soil used it on the Normandy coast prior to Operation Overlord. On New Year's Eve 1943, Logan Scott-Bowden, R.E. landed a boat on the beach at Ver-sur-Mer to take samples of sand, so as to dispel doubts on the feasibility of landing British tanks there. There was no moon on the night chosen but it was also thought that the guards would be distracted by the Festive Season. Unfortunately the lighthouse was exceptionally beaming out its light in celebration.

The frogman related how he was forced to coordinate his advance to the rhythm of its rays. A few months later Davis' equipment was used in maintenance on the prefabricated ports and when refloating sunken ships. Lionel Crabb used the Davis apparatus.

As did the Germans, the Italians and later the French, all of whom were involved in perfecting the gear now used by amateur and professional divers the world over. Advances made in times of war made for further development equally for underwater industrial applications as for science.

The vast ranged of accessories are worthy of note: diving suits, pressure reducers, depth finders, sound equipment ... and, of course, calculators, which made longer and deeper diving both possible and safer. It is in the composition of the gas inhaled; a mixture of helium, hydrogen and oxygen that the most significant progress has been achieved.

Divers in active service with Davis respiratory and exhalatory recycling equipment.

Air-sea rescue

Life-saving precautions have always been a preoccupation aboard ships, for passengers and crew. Air-sea rescue is a more recent development, notably with regard to the specific needs for retrieving pilots forced to bail out. Pilots are far more precious than a plane and the treasures of ingenuity included devices to keep them alive.

Almost all aircraft were equipped with inflatable dinghies with: first aid, drinks, chocolate, an unsinkable knife, distress signals, flares, a fluorescent substance which leaves a green trail in the dinghy's wake, a mirror, a footing anchor, a flag, a whistle and a transmitter to facilitate location. All these items were lightweight and took up little space.

Inflated life raft fitted with solar. Still and condensation system to produce fresh water.

During the last war, the main problem was water supply. Two solutions were adopted: one chemical, developed by the British Admiralty, the other by evaporation, a system perfected in the USA.

The chemical method made use of mixed ions of silver and baryon which, associated with charcoal transformed the chloride and sulphate in sea water into insoluble salt, hence transforming the sea water into fresh water after filtering. The device in each dinghy measured 10 x 10 x 15 cm, and was capable of producing 5 times its volume in water, i.e. 2.5 litres. Several hundred thousands of these kits were issued to the RAF.

The American device was composed of a solar still containing sponges, which, when soaked in sea water, mounted in a plastic balloon and, when exposed to the sun, induced condensation that filled a container and cooled in contact with cold sea water to produce fresh water.

A few lifeboats came ashore on the coasts of Normandy and the French Resistance first hid their occupants, then arranged their passage along the escape routes to safety.

The RAF estimated that its Air Sea Rescue Service, along with the rapid intervention of Royal Navy launches, saved 3,305 crew members, i.e. almost one in two. Air-sea rescue today has profited from the aforementioned developments, together with more recent advances, notably systems of detection-localisation by satellite: Argos, GPS, etc.

The midget submarine

Two Americans, David Bushell with his Turtle in 1775 during the War of Independence, used to torpedo English ships in New York harbour, and Robert Fulton with his Nautilus in 1798, were the forerunners of the concept of the midget submarine.

British Midget Submarine X23 off Ouistreham.

Robert Fulton came to offer his Nautilus to the 'Directoire' in France, at the time at war with England. The small 6 metre-long and appr. 2 metres in diameter submarine was displayed in Le Havre in 1800, Brest in 1801, then in Paris on the Seine; however, it failed to draw Napoleon's interest.

On the 22nd of May 1878, John Philip Holland launched the USA's first midget submarine. The Tzar also produced a submarine, at first with pedals then, in 1904, with an electric engine.

It was only at the end of the First World War that midget submarines were used in action, when, in 1918, the Italians attacked the Austrian fleet in Trieste.

Curiously enough, neither the Russians, the forerunners, the Americans, nor the French made use of the midget submarine during the Second World War. It was the Japanese, the Italians and above all the British who put flotillas of them into service – the British Class X 'Midgets' that took soundings and bearings on the Calvados coast to draw up the marine charts for Operation Neptune. The tiny cabin: 1.6.m x 1.3m x 2.5m, could squeeze in 3 to 5 men.

This was also true of the X20 Exemplar and the X23 Xiphas that reconnoitred the Anglo-Canadian landing beaches. The X20 berthed submerged off Courseulles to the west and the X23 at Ouistreham to the east, as from the 4th of June, awaiting the order for the Landings. On 6th of June, still submerged, they put out their goniometrical markings to guide the Allied ships to their respective beaches. Had Operation Neptune been called off, these two submarines could not have returned to England. They were to be scuttled and the crews to go ashore disguised as civilians with 'real' fake papers and ration cards.

With stupefaction, the Allies discovered, after the war, that the Germans had a fleet of 50 midget submarines at Kiel copied from a British Midget captured at Kaafiord (Norway).

They were submarines of the Seehund type, also used by the French Navy up to the late 1950s. Today, Midget submarines no longer appear to be used by the world's navies. The knowledge gained in their development has been used to build craft for underwater exploration. On the 15th of February 1954, Picard's Belgian FNRS – remodelled by the CNRS – descended down to the Ocean bed to a depth of 4,050 metres. Later, both the American Alvin and the French Nautilus dived 6,000 metres.

It was the three-man crew Nautilus, with its 'mother' ship the Nadir, developed by IFREMER, that discovered the wreck of the Titanic at a depth of 4,426 metres, on the 1st of September 1985.

The Victor, the first tele-operated and guided non-crew submarine today, complements the Nautilus. It can operate 24 hours a day for several days.

Surgery

Five hundred years before our era, Hippocrates the father of Medicine said, 'If thou aspirest to become a surgeon, join the Army and follow it everywhere.' Warfare is the making of medicine and, in short spaces of time, great progress has been made to the benefit of humankind in general.

New medicine: penicillin, sulphonamides, streptomycin, etc, blood transfusion and plasma, methods of anaesthesia and reanimation, new surgical techniques and new surgical implements used by army surgeons have combined to reduce by half the number of deaths among the wounded in the two 20th century world wars.

American Surgical Assistance Jeep in the bocage, Normandy.

Surgeons operated close to the front line in the 600 hospitals and 40,000 beds that had been established in Normandy.

Anaesthesia was revolutionised entirely by the use of penthotal, which was also used to treat war neurosis. Penthotal is also used notably for narcotic analysis and for epidurals.

Reanimation techniques have also been facilitated, notably with the use of oxygen. Treatment of burns by grafting skin has been made possible thanks to the use of dermatome, which enables healthy skin to be taken for grafting.

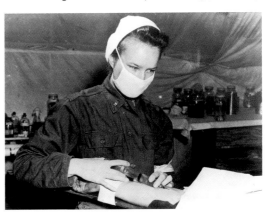

Surgery on the front lines in Normandy.

Facial plastic surgery has thus been able to limit the number of disfigurements that were so difficult to treat in the First World War. All these new techniques, as well as those still to be proven, were in the hands of army surgeons.

To take account of the point surgery had reached at the time of the Landings, it should be mentioned that the US surgeon Blalock operated the first time ever in 1944 – a malformation of the heart, coined with the term 'Blue'.

HEALTH

DDT

DDT Dichloro-diphenil-trichloroethane was discovered in 1873 and used in dyeworks. In 1939, P. Müller and H. Martin, who worked for Geigy, a Swiss company established in Bâle, discovered the value of DDT as an insecticide, when studying its effect on potatoes. This major discovery earned P. Müller the Nobel Prize in Medicine in 1948.

P. Müller.

DDT was first patented in Switzerland in 1940, in Great Britain in 1942 and, thirdly, in the USA in 1943. The use of DDT in the army was of great importance and this inexpensive and easy to produce insecticide was referred to as the 'Saviour of Mankind', a term that was literally true, since it is estimated to have saved 25 million lives across the globe.

Military uniforms were impregnated with insecticide (as they had been earlier in the war against gas). In Equatorial zones where malaria-carrying mosquitoes were prevalent, areas of water and swamp were sprayed from the air. In December 1943 and January 1944, a typhus epidemic in Naples was kept in check; by treating 1,300,000 Neapolitans.

Eradication of mosquito larvae by British troops.

During the 1944 Landings, Allied troops had cartons of DDT powder in their kits. Aerosols capable of disinfecting 28 cubic metres were also issued. Impregnated battledress – which remained so even after being cleaned several times, still retained the smell of insecticide.

In 1945 DDT, was used to eradicate lice in concentration camps. Unfortunately, the miracle insecticide had side effects on the environment, largely due to its lasting effects. Traces of DDT were found in fish, birds and animals in places as far afield as Australia. It is estimated that of the 3 million tonnes of DDT produced, half are still active. A million tonnes are still present in the sea, worldwide.

In 1973, industrial nations finally prohibited the production of DDT.

Penicillin

In a dispatch to the 'London Gazette' on the 3rd of September 1946, Field Marshall Montgomery wrote, 'Another interesting fact is that in the last war, of those with stomach wounds, two out of three died. Surgical units operating just behind the front line have now reduced this danger, In the Normandy campaign, two out of three survived. The survival rate has been revolutionised by the use of penicillin.' It is usual to attribute this breakthrough to Alexander Fleming, the British bacteriologist who discovered penicillin in 1928. The British writer Richard Barry attributes the discovery to a Frenchman, Ernest Duchesne, who had evidence in his research of the antibiotic qualities of 'Penicillium glaucum' in 1897 in Lyon.

A. Fleming.

Whoever it was and independently of the aforementioned research, Fleming, who like all the biologists of his time, was looking for a cure for influenza, indeed discovered

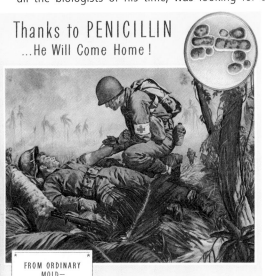

'Penicillium rubrum', which is of the same family as 'Penicillium album' and is present in the fermentation of certain cheeses. This substance arrested the proliferation of bacteria since it secreted an anti-microbial agent which is now called penicillin. Since not yet stabilised and not exactly what he was looking for, it was not immediately considered to be 'the magic remedy', and its use was consequently delayed for a long time.

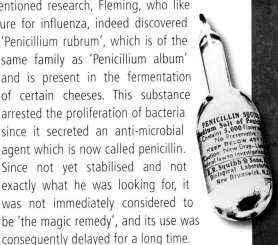

It was Howard Florey, a professor at Oxford who, in 1938, succeeded in stabilising penicillin. Two years later, B. Chain, also at Oxford, produced a purer substance, identifiable as an antibiotic that could be used on humans in clinical settings. Fleming, Florey and Chain all received the Nobel Prize for medicine in 1945. The appearance of penicillin complemented the use of sulphonamides, which were beginning to show their limitations and side-effects.

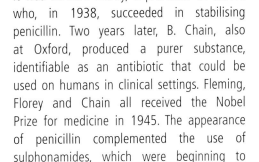

HEALTH

Streptomycin

A biologist by the name of S.A. Waksman, from the Department of Agriculture at Rutger's University, New Brunswick had, since 1910, specialised in bacteria present in the soil.

In 1940, he noticed that tuberculosis bacilli present in the soil were disappearing and concluded that other hostile germs were responsible. He therefore invented the term 'antibiotic' – 'a substance produced by a micro-organism capable of inhibiting or destroying other micro-organisms'.

S.A. Waksman.

In 1942, among others engaged in research, he discovered streptomycin: particularly active against bacilli in tuberculosis. He entrusted to one of his colleagues, A. Schatz, the task of segregating streptomycin, which was achieved in 1943. S.A. Waksman was awarded the Nobel Prize in 1952.

Was streptomycin used as an antibiotic with sulphonamides and penicillin by the American Army Medical Corps? Some say it was used in Normandy in 1944, others claim it was not available until 1945. One thing is certain – research published by Schatz in 1944, the release of which may have been delayed by the US authorities in order to keep it under wraps.

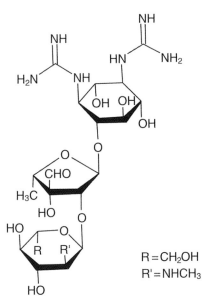

$R = CH_2OH$
$R' = NHCH_3$

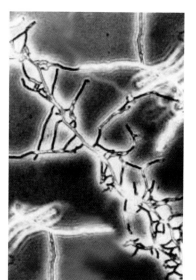

We also know that France received 92 kilos of this precious medication for hospital use in 1945.

HEALTH

Sulphonamides

From 1932 to 1935, the German biochemist Paul Domagk methodically studied thousands of chemical agents to assess their antibacterial properties. He discovered that Prontosil, a red pigment used for painting, first made in 1905 and of therapeutic value, could in fact prove useful against streptococci when its formula was slightly modified. He tested his findings on his daughter, who was suffering from a life-threatening streptococcus infection – she recovered.

G. Domagk.

Domagk published his discovery and the medical profession found many uses for sulphonamide. In 1936, the remedy proved remarkably successful in checking an epidemic of meningitis that had broken out among French Foreign Legion troops in Algeria.

Paul Domagk was awarded the Nobel Prize for Medicine in 1939, but deprived of it by Hitler – he could finally benefit from his prize in 1947.

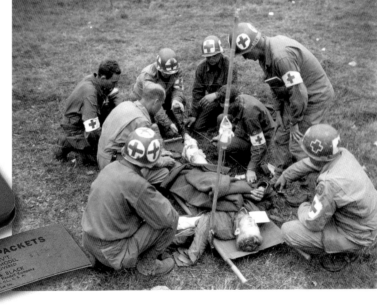

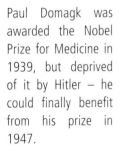

During the D-Day Landings, all GIs were issued with a First Aid Pouch, which was worn on their belts and contained a packet of sulphonamide powder inside a metal box with a red seal.

Blood transfusion

At the beginning of the 20th century, an Austrian, Karl Landstreimer identified blood groups, which reduced accidents during transfusion. He was awarded the Nobel Prize in 1930. Although reduced in numbers, accidents still occurred and, in 1940, Landstreimer identified the rhesus factor, which completed compatibility criteria between donors and receivers.

As from the outbreak of hostilities, Britain and the USA created blood banks to store blood and plasma, in their natural state or dehydrated. Each had different uses. Plasma was used to treat burns and to re-establish a satisfactory level, close to that of blood, to ensure correct circulation pending hospital admission.

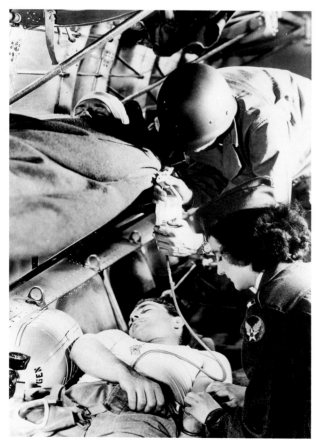

Blood transfusion on the front lines.

Liquid or dehydrated plasma was available in all First Aid Posts near the front line. Blood, the correct state of which was maintained by an anti-coagulant, was stored in special flasks and refrigerated at a temperature of 4°C. Blood collection was particularly well organised.

The USA could count on up to 240,000 donors in one day. Blood banks in Britain and America each had a stock of almost 10,000 litres of available fresh blood, pending the launch of the D-Day Landings, to which a daily complement of nearly 1,000 litres was added.

A daily liaison between the USA and blood banks in Britain was ensured by refrigerated four-engine Douglas Skymaster freight planes. Also on a daily basis, fast light aircraft crossed the Channel with isotherm containers. Today, you can still sometimes find them for sale in car-boot sales along the Normandy coast. Blood-related logistics did not stop there. Blood transfusion was of primary importance for the Allied Forces. Special convoys were escorted by Sherman tanks. Blood was even dropped by parachute when needed, in refrigerated containers, for the Normandy Landings took place during the summer. Supplies of blood were, on occasion, even fired over the lines in shells, notably at Mortain.

Blood stored in isotherm flasks.

A vaccine against influenza

Following the great epidemics of Spanish Flu in 1918 and 1919 that accounted for 20 and 40 million deaths, i.e. more than the two world wars reunited, the Americans decided to look for a vaccine with which they could inoculate their GIs prior to their return to Europe. During the great pandemic, 800,000 of their soldiers had contracted flu and 23,000 had died, a figure in excess of losses in action in France at the time.

Of the three American researchers working on the virus, W.M. Stanley was first to identify the flu virus and was awarded the Nobel Prize in 1946. Another American, J.E. Salk, perfected the first anti-viral vaccine in 1933. It was only in 1942 that American and Canadian research led to the cultivation of the virus in the allantoic fluid of embryonic eggs.

W.M. Stanley.

In 1943, it was discovered that there were at least three types of virus: A, B and C, each with a sub-virus AO, A1, A2, ... and that the spectrum of the vaccine had to be enlarged. Just as important

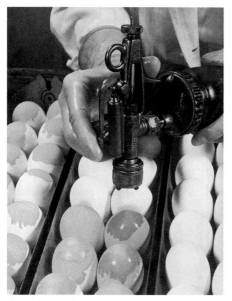

The culture of virus in eggs.

as the vaccine's discovery, an industrial method for mass producing added a further challenge. Millions and millions of fertile eggs were needed since the method consisted in placing a microscopic quantity of virus in the air-pocket of each fertilised egg. Two to three days later, around a tablespoonful of virus could be taken from each egg.

In this way, from a batch of 150,000 eggs, some 1,000 litres of virus could be used to produce the vaccine. An entire international network was set up to keep watch on influenza virus propagation.

In an attempt to find an explanation for the outbreak of the 1918-1919 epidemic, the recent examination of the lungs of a 22-year-old American soldier who died 80 years earlier, revealed a virus of the type H1N1, similar to that of swine influenza, transmissible to man. The bodies of miners were also exhumed in the north of Norway, in the hope that the virus would lie dormant in the cold and could therefore be identified.

Vitamins

In the course of his famous voyage round the world in 1740, Lord Anson lost over half his crew who went down with scurvy.

In 1770, Captain Cook discovered that his sailors recovered from scurvy if they ate citrus fruit (notably limes). The famous captain had, unintentionally, discovered vitamins. On his return to London, he submitted a report to the Admiralty, noting his observation and, on the 7th of March 1777, in a communication to the Royal Society he mentioned the useful role of citrus fruit.

F.G. Hopkins.

Forty years later, the Admiralty included barrels of lime juice in naval rations. It took over 100 years to dispose of shipowners' objections and, in 1894, the Board of Trade applied the same obligation to the British Merchant Service.

The Army, whilst acknowledging the need to eat citrus fruit, especially after the Crimean War, pretexted the difficulties involved in transporting barrels of fruit juice. It was only in 1906 that Sir Frederick Gowlnd Hopkins discovered mysterious substances in food, termed 'accessory food factors' to which he gave the name of vitamins. He was awarded the Nobel Prize in 1929.

In 1928 a Hungarian, Szent-Györgyi, discovered ascorbic acid – vitamin C – in lemons. Haworth in England and Hirst at Reichstein in Switzerland both succeeded in producing a synthetic version in 1933. With artificial vitamins that were totally identical to the original, the Army need not transport barrels, but could issue tablets to provide vitamins for the troops.

The first tablets were despatched during the Siege of Tobruk in 1941, to ensure the garrison survived pending the arrival of reinforcements, thanks to these vitamin lozenges, which consequently came to be called 'Tobruk Tablets'. The RAF also issued pilots with a cocktail of vitamins A and B to augment their acuteness of vision. At different times, other vitamins were discovered – those soluble in water or fat: C and B... and others – A, D and E. The role of vitamins has been important enough for the Nobel Foundation to award prizes to no fewer than 8 scientists involved in their development.

In occupied France, when children suffered from malnutrition, 'Marshal Pétain Biscuits' containing vitamins were distributed in schools. In Normandy, the Allies also distributed vitamin-supplemented chocolate to children. Later, they did likewise in Paris, then in Marseilles. The Red Cross joined them by distributing vitamin-supplemented jam to around a million other children.

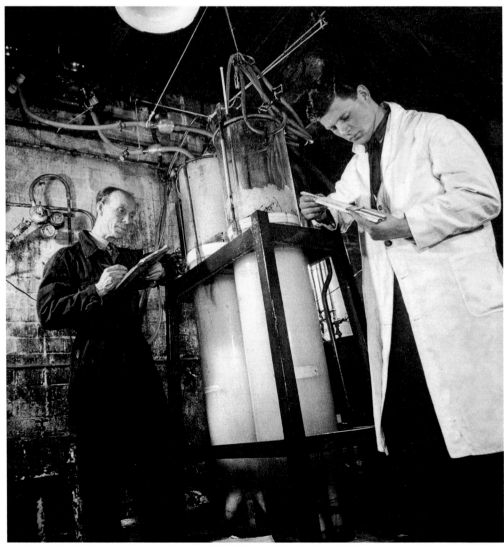

Vitamin A generator in Britain – August 1944.

Jet aircraft

At the beginning of the 20th century, France held a dominant position in aeronautic development. 'Aviators' from all over the world flocked to France to exchange ideas, meet with others, perfect and try out these machines that were heavier than air. Among them: Blériot,

Heinkel 178 in 1939.

Wright, Farman, Santos-Dumont, Roland Garros and Lübbe, all innovators, there was also a young French engineer, René Lorin, who had thought up a new method of propulsion that would replace both the heavy thermal engine and the propeller. He described his jet-propelled engine in the *L'Aérophile* magazine 1st September 1908 issue. He had developed a new system of propulsion with an exhaust engine: the stato-reactor, for which he filed a patent in 1913.

During the First World War, René Lorin wanted to build a pilotless jet plane, equipped with a gyroscope and a barometric altimeter to bomb enemy targets. He had therefore anticipated the Second World War's V1 rocket. However, considered excessively innovative, no one paid an interest in his projects. Dispirited, Lorin compiled all his theories in a book entitled, *L'Air et la Vitesse* (Air and Speed), published in 1930 by Editions Chiron. The book mainly attracted interest among Germans engaged in research!

The principle of jet-propulsion was not however, new. The Chinese and the Greeks knew about propulsion by gunpowder and by gas. Children the world over, knew that a deflating balloon is propelled by the outrush of air. In Germany, in 1928, F. von Opel flew the first jet rocket-propelled plane in history, for several seconds. The same year, a 23-year-old cadet RAF officer, Frank Whittle, described a new system of jet-propulsion capable of powering an aircraft in his thesis. The device consisted of a compressor, an expansion chamber and a turbine. The era of turbojet propulsion had begun.

In January 1930, Whittle obtained his first patent and, in 1936, he filed a second patent for a turbofan engine. The same year, with private capital, the PowerJet Company, set up the first turbojet with a Whittle compressor that had operated on the test bench on the 12th of April 1937.

Concurrently, the Germans, despite having started later, achieved their aim sooner. Indeed, von Ohain, who was working with Heinkel, constructed a jet plane and, for 8 minutes, successfully flew the first turbojet – the HE 178 – on the 27th of August 1939. Germany remained at the forefront until the end of the war.

Arado 234 taking off in 1944.

During the 1940s, Rolls Royce, on the one hand, and BMW, Heinkel and Junkers, on the other hand, developed a number of jet-propelled aircraft and equipped respectively: the Gloster Meteor, the Heinkel 162, the Messerschmitt 262, then the Arado 234 C – the World's first four-engined jet, which first flew in February 1944. All technological features had been perfected, down to the ceramics on the Junker engines! In 40 years, Europe had invented, to the finest detail, the jet-propelled plane.

Today, all the firms mentioned above continue to thrive and are partners in the Airbus Consortium except one, Arado. In actual fact, its Chairman Heinrich Lübbe, a friend of Roland Garros in the early part of the century, refused to join the Nazi Party and his firm was nationalised, later to be liquidated when the regime collapsed. Now, where is the moral in that story? Let's return to Normandy in the summer of 1944: the Allied bridgehead was firmly established.

Late July, the German GHQ sent out their system V reconnaissance aircraft, the invulnerable twin-engined Jet Arado 234, to photograph all Allied positions. The mission, on the 2nd of August, took its pilot, Erich Sommer, into hostile territory for the very first time. He flew three times over Normandy and brought back dozens of remarkable photographs that laid bare the entire Allied logistics.

The conquest of space

On the 13th of June 1944, when the Allies were consolidating their bridgehead in Normandy, just one week after the Landings, the first V1 was fired at midnight and fell on London.

A few hours later, a V2 went out of control and came down in a marsh near Kalmar in Sweden. The country, though neutral, promptly handed over what remained of it to the Allies, after a rather bizarre journey in a hearse, it reached the west, avoiding German attempts to recuperate it.

The era of missiles had begun – the V1 and V2, though very different in design, led to the conquest of space. The V1, brought into service by the *Luftwaffe*, (German Air Force) was a small pilotless plane. Catapulted from a reinforced concrete ramp, aimed at its target, it was powered by an Argus pulsejet engine. The idea had been taken from the book by René Lorin. The V1 flew at 600 km/h with a range of 250 km. Designed by Fieseler, 22,000 of them were built by Volkswagen at a unit cost of 600 US Dollars in current value.

A V1 about to be completed in a German underground factory.

The V2 was a missile powered by a propellant – a mixture of oxygen and alcohol. It took off vertically, was put into service by the German Army and fired by the artillery. Just like the V1, it was guided by a gyroscope and could not be put off course by counter electronic devices. It was largely supersonic and reached an altitude of 85 km, and boasted a range of 350 km. In weapons it was the absolute must. First fired successfully on the 3rd of October 1942, ten thousand more were produced.

The potential targets in the UK had to be within 250 km for the V1 and 350 km for the V2. If, from identified targets such as London, Aldershot, Bristol, Southampton or Winchester, we draw circle. of 250 km and 350 km in diameter, the southern circumferences take in the north of the Cotentin peninsula and the Seine Maritime department. Considering the presence of depots and liquid oxygen production plants, it is understandable why Normandy played such an important role in the use of German V missiles. There were 65 V1

V2 preparing for blast off.

TRANSPORT AND LOGISTICS

sites in Cotentin and 116 in Seine Maritime. The precise location of all V2 sites is unsure for, with the exception of a few large bunkers like Brécourt and depots such as Hautmesnil, south of Caen, or those by liquid gas stocks, other launchpads were merely in the form of reinforced concrete ramps near a railway line, of which Le Molay Littry is a fine example.

It should be remembered that the development of these weapons cost the lives of some 20,000 deportees in the Dora and Laura camps in underground factories that were never bombed, near Buchenwald. Their work was directed by the Nazi, Wilhelm von Braun, who later became an American citizen!

After the war, the Americans 'recovered' 118 scientists, 250 complete V2s and hundreds of tonnes of material that was shipped to the USA from Cherbourg. Everything left on site was destroyed so that the Russians would find nothing. In spite of this, the latter gathered enough material to reconstitute almost 1,000 V2s. How many scientists were taken to the USSR is not known. The Americans successfully fired their first V2 in the desert of New Mexico on the 3rd of March 1946. But it was the Russians who came out best with these spoils of war. On the 4th of October 1957, they launched the Sputnik, generated worldwide stupefaction.

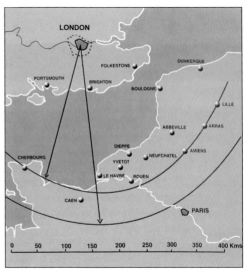

Rocket sites from which it was possible to reach London. V1: 250 km. V2: 350 km.

The competition that followed is well known. On the 20th of July 1969, the Americans first set foot on the Moon.

Europe was running behind, but with the Ariane 'family', direct descendants of the V2, it succeeded in catching up, also with the help of German scientists. It may be noted that the propeller was produced at Vernon in Normandy. From the cost in lives to the cost at the time in cash, weaponry in US Dollars:
- V1/V2: 3,000 million
- Radar (USA): 3,000 million
- Atomic bomb (Manhattan Project): 2,000 million

The Dakota

Another example of early invention and late development is the DC-3 or Dakota: a transport plane designed in the early thirties, offering a concentration of innovation and that still flies today.

In the early thirties, air travel was in its very early days, and aircraft offered passengers very basic comfort. Finding no suitable planes on the market, TWA asked Douglas to design a new passenger plane capable of comfortably carrying 12 passengers.

In 1933, Donald Douglas, Kindelberger and Arthur Raymond brought out a plane with startling innovations. It had a metal frame reinforced by stressed skin fuselage, rendering the craft 'fail safe'. The DC-1 was born.

Only one plane was made, but its remarkable qualities appeared in a larger version, the DC-2 which flew under TWA colours. Douglas assured them that the aircraft had a life of 75,000 hours, namely over ten times that of its competitors. History would prove him right.

Following the DC-2's first commercial flights, the famous DC-3 was designed and the first test flight was conducted on the 17th of December 1935 in Santa Monica. The Aircraft was put into service by the U.S. Army as the C47 and by the Royal Air Force as the Dakota.

A Dakota taking off with a glider in tow.

TRANSPORT AND LOGISTICS

With a wingspan of 29 metres and a length of 19.5 metres, it boasted a range of 2,600 km. Originally it had 1,000 hp twin-engines. It could carry 21, and later 27 passengers or 4 tonnes of freight at a speed of 340 km/h. Made entirely of metal, it was the first mass-produced plane with an automatic pilot, the Sperry gyroscope. It cost $90,000.

During the Normandy Landings, the DC-3 was the quintessential multipurpose plane. At dawn on the 6th of June, hundreds of them dropped thousands of paratroops who, complete with equipment, were 18 to an aircraft and landed on the east and west flanks of the bridgehead. DC-3s also acted as tug planes for Waco-CG 4A (15 men) or Horsa (20 men) gliders. They were used later to bring in equipment and mail, transporting the wounded on their return journey. Some were used in precision drops and were fitted with 'Mickey' radar to identify their objectives. A few were based at the airfield in Saint Aubin d'Arquenay from where they towed back recuperated gliders to the UK and took part in the unfortunate Operation Market Garden on the 17th of September 1944.

Finally, they acted as transport planes ferrying goods to besieged Berlin during the embargo imposed by the Soviets in 1948. Civil airlines took delivery of 800 DC-3's whilst 10,928 were built for use by the Armed Forces, compared to a grand total of 675,000 aircraft used by belligerents from all nations engaged in the Second World War.

Dakotas ready to tow gliders.

Reservoirs at the Château de Saint-Gabriel.

In 1900, Alexander, a young Scot aged 9 years attending Clifton College Bristol took German and French, Latin and Greek. That is quite a lot for a youngster and Pindar's Ode to Nature went unlearned. It was less pardonable however, since Alexander's class had recently visited Bath, a few miles away and on the front of the pump-room at the Roman Baths, the first verse that he should have learned was engraved, ARISTON MEN UDOR, (greatest, however, [is] water), taken in the sense that from water, flows life itself. Alexander was given a hundred lines of that very text, which he never forgot. He had a distinguished career: first as lieutenant in the engineers during the First World War and later as a civil engineer. He returned to the Royal Engineers in 1939 and the 1944 Landings took his unit, the 13th Airfield Construction Group, ashore at Ver-sur-Mer. He was now Colonel A.C. Rankin and his task was to construct temporary airfields where Allied aircraft could land from 11th June onwards. He was first positioned at Crépon from where he moved to Coulombs, the site destined to become the key Allied air base. It was summer and, despite the poor weather, clouds of dust rose through the steel-netted runways whenever planes took off. A target for the enemy, the dust spelt danger to aircraft engines too. Planned since January 1943,

Lt Colonel A.C. Rankin, OBE, MC, BEC, Royal Engineers.

the 'Water Scheme' was aimed at spraying the runways in order to settle the dust; however, priority was placed on providing drinking water for the troops. The lesson of the Libyan campaign had

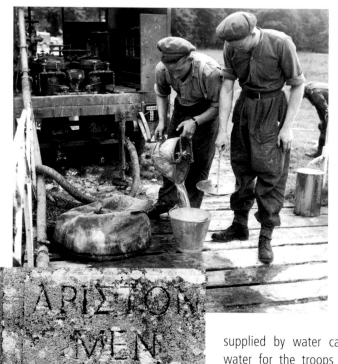

'Water is Best'. An R.E. Pumping Station built at Saint-Gabriel.

been well learnt: 'A battle may be lost for lack of a glass of water.' The Water Scheme made provision for a double supply of water: both for drinking and for operational purposes. First supplies were brought in from the UK in 'Jerrycans', then in tanks, which were soon to be replaced by some twenty wells, dug out immediately after the Landings on sites provided by geologists in Normandy.

In addition, water from neighbouring rivers and streams was collected, filtered and sterilised before being supplied by water cart or via pipes. From drinking water for the troops we move to the second phase of the 'Water Scheme'; a functional water supply, the implementation of which was entrusted to Colonel Rankin, among others.

Around fifteen pumping stations were set up along waterways; basins and sterilisation stations were built and miles of pipes laid, through which millions of cubic feet of water were brought in to be sprayed every night on airfield runways, in order to settle the dust. What now remains of this gigantic two-fold water supply: enough drinking water to quench thirst and enough industrial water to make France's water giant, Veolia, go green with envy. A few wells are still in use, and miles of underground piping with three permanent pumping stations still remain. One bears the inscription B.L.A. for British Liberation Army, another CARPE DIEM and the third ARISTON MEN UDOR. Alexander had learned his lesson!

This last station also pumped the water flowing from the Verrine fountain in Saint Gabriel.

Colonel A.C. Rankin completed his mission by constructing an airfield in record time, for Montgomery to enter Germany. The latter congratulated him and recommended him to H.M. King George VI to receive the OBE (Order of the British Empire).

To illustrate certain effects of the Earth's rotation as described by Newton 100 years previously, Léo Foucault produced a device that rotated at speed which he described as a 'gyroscope'. The direction of the axis of rotation is unaffected by the movement of its base. It is this property that constitutes the unswerving direction of the gyroscope. In 1875, the Brit, Henry Bessemer, and the German, Otto Schlick, used pig iron as ballast in ships. In the early 20th century, the German, Hermann Anschütz, and the American, Elmer A. Sperry, used the gyroscopic principle to invent a compass for ships, the magnetic needle of which could not be deflected by the electro-magnetic field created by the proximity of metal. They had invented the gyrocompass.

Sperry automatic pilot.

The use to which this innovation was applied in 1912 to aeroplanes brought fame to its inventor. E.A. Sperry was an engineer and an American University of Cornell graduate. His son, Lawrence, exhibited a Curtiss seaplane in 1914 in Paris, with an automatic pilot. He took off, put his arms above his head, with his passenger standing on the wings, creating quite a sensation.

In 1917, Sperry fitted up gyroscopic torpedoes to be fired from aircraft and perfected the gyrocompass. In 1935, DC-3s were the first planes to be fitted with an automatic pilot.

A gyroscope toy.

The course of the Second World War saw the advent of guided missiles, V1 and V2, guided bombs and torpedoes and many guided planes, one of which was the Arado 234. All had gyroscopic equipment.

Since, many different types of gyroscopic guided aircraft equipment have emerged, in ever smaller and more sophisticated versions: laser driven and complementary to satellite navigation GPS (Global Positioning System).

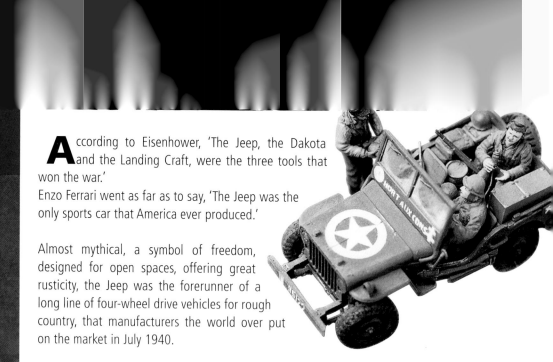

According to Eisenhower, 'The Jeep, the Dakota and the Landing Craft, were the three tools that won the war.'

Enzo Ferrari went as far as to say, 'The Jeep was the only sports car that America ever produced.'

Almost mythical, a symbol of freedom, designed for open spaces, offering great rusticity, the Jeep was the forerunner of a long line of four-wheel drive vehicles for rough country, that manufacturers the world over put on the market in July 1940.

The U.S. Army requested that some hundred firms develop a reconnaissance vehicle suitable for rough country. A delay of 49 days, with a maximum price of $175,000 was allowed to firms submitting offers. Bantam replied, along with Willys and Ford and was accepted at the figure of $171,185 and 75 cents! The Jeep (from G.P.: General Purpose), designed by K. Prost from Bantam, was born.

De Gaulle on the Beach between Courseulles and Graye-sur-Mer on 16th June 1944.

Jeep crossing Bretteville-l'Orgueilleuse in the summer of 1944.

Willys and Ford came in later and joined Bantam to produce the famous four-wheel drive model. Mass production began from 1941 at the Willys Factory in Toledo, where a vehicle worth $750 was produced in the record time of 1 minute 20 seconds. The Jeep's baptism of fire was in Burma in 1942. A total of 640,000 of these vehicles were produced throughout the war.

During the Normandy Landings, the first Jeeps came down in gliders, followed by thousands and thousands unloaded from ships. Assembly workshops were even set up in the Normandy bocage, hence creating an annexe of Detroit, somewhere in the midst of the Normandy countryside. On the 14th of June, the first cases of component parts were unloaded at Arromanches and, from the 16th of June, the first Jeeps 'made in Normandy' left their assembly lines under the apple trees. Local productivity reached 100 Jeeps and 20 lorries daily.

When issued to them, the British nicknamed the Jeep, the 'pneumonia car' since it was so draughty, but it was aboard a Jeep that one of them, from the 3rd Infantry Division, first drove into Caen on the morning of the 9th of July 1944.

Almost a quarter of a million Jeeps were destroyed during the war and nearly 400,000 were sold in different countries. It was adopted in Normandy for all sorts of farm work, from towing farm machinery to collecting milk. Today, it is not unusual to see one on the road, in addition to those now in the hands of collectors and connoisseurs.

The Liberty Ship

As German submarines sank increasing numbers of British ships in the Atlantic, Britain, facing such emergency, ordered from the United States – still a neutral country – ocean-going merchant ships that could be mass-produced.

On the strength of this 'shipping order' and conscious of the vulnerability of their own merchant fleet, a shipbuilding project was put in hand for ocean-going cargo ships of an improved type, called E.C.2, (Emergency Cargo ship 2).

The Liberty Ship was born; it joined its legendary Second World War companions, the jeep and the DC-3.

Hence, the USA, long before Pearl Harbor, and for the first time anywhere, standardised the building of merchant ships of 10,800 tonnes, 135 metres in length, equipped with 2,500 hp engines and reaching a speed of 11 knots.

The E.C.2 programme included the building of 3,148 vessels from 1941 to 1945. Eighteen shipyards were approved, 7 of which were controlled by J.H. Kaiser, champion of the new concepts of accelerated shipbuilding.

In various factories, 19,000 different components were made and sent to the shipyards for assembly. Among other innovations, the Liberty Ship was welded throughout. Each workman wore a belt with compartments for all the necessary tools. Each workstation provided different gases and tools for welding and drilling, attached to appropriate supports. A merchant ship was built in 30 days on average. The first Liberty Ship was launched, incomplete, on the 27th of September 1941. After the Pearl Harbor attack on the 7th of December 1941, things speeded up. The race against time resulted in many imperfections. It was also decided to build a ship at such speed as to dissuade competitors.

It was J.H. Kaiser's yard that met the challenge. Liberty Ship No 440, baptised *Robert E. Peary*, was put on the stocks on the 8th of November 1942. She was launched on the 11th and sailed on the 15th. It had taken only four days, 15 hours and 25 minutes to assemble her. She sailed until June

en 4 jours, 15 heures, et 25 minutes

LA CONSTRUCTION D'UN NAVIRE MARCHAND

Launched by *R.E. Peary* On 8th November 1942 at Richmond, USA.

1963 when she was scrapped. Kaiser had won hands down, though record building times varied considerably from yard to yard. Some, for example, had no slipway. There is an account of how one sponsor, arriving shortly before the launch, was amazed to see a bottle of champagne but no ship. He was told that, although she was indeed a little late, she wouldn't be long! A total of 2,710 Liberty Ships were built. Around 200 were sunk. A few proved to have defects in their welding or demonstrated a lack of buoyancy in comparison to ships with a traditional riveted hull.

An array of Liberty Ships were to be seen off the Normandy coast from the 6th of June 1944 onwards. Eight of them were towed in to be sunk to form the breakwater for Gooseberry 1 & 2, three at Utah and four at Omaha. Germany artillery tried but failed to sink them prior to their arrival at the planned position.

Among the hundreds of Liberty Ships that shuttled between the Channel coasts, *Jeremiah O'Brien* which made 12 crossings between Southampton and Utah Beach in the summer of 1944, and *John W. Brown*, are the only vessels still afloat. *Jeremiah O'Brien* stopped over in Cherbourg in 1994.

As part of the lend-lease treaty, signed in 1946, France received 75 Liberty Ships, 30 of which were given names connected with the Battle of Normandy: *Argentan, Avranches, Bayeux, Bernières, Caen, Cherbourg, Courseulles, Coutances, Domfront, Falaise, Grandcamp, Granville, Isigny, Le Havre, Les Andelys, Lisieux, Mortain, Ouistreham, Pont-Audemer, Pont-L'Évêque, Port-en-Bessin, Rouen, Sainte-Mère-Église, Saint-Lô, Saint-Marcouf, Saint Valéry, Troarn, Valognes, Ville du Havre, Vire.*

A Liberty ship lying off Vierville.

Superstar logistics

Logistics: 'The careful organisation of a complicated activity so that it happens in a successful and effective way,' as the Cambridge Dictionary has it.

To put in place the logistics of Operation Overlord was so considerable and complex that a few lines of explanation are necessary.

The countdown began in April 1942, following the Boléro Conference in London when it was decided to cross the Channel and put an end to the German domination of Europe. A start was made and two years were needed to prepare the plan, train the necessary troops and assemble material which had to be constructed and even invented, not forgetting working out lines of communication... Eisenhower arrived in London in June 1942, to prepare the American contribution to the programme.

It concerned the transport of 2 million men, 500,000 vehicles, together with millions of tonnes of food, petrol and ammunition!

Nearly 7,000 ships were needed, most of which were purpose-built. They were to sail through five lanes marked out port and starboard and kept continuously swept of mines. Having obtained the relevant maps and charts, these had to be updated. In order to find convenient 'hards' for landing, frogmen were sent out to record declivity and to take samples of sand on the beaches. From these findings, nearly 200 million navigation charts were printed.

12 tonnes of equipment and supplies arrived with each GI.

Beaches marked out for landing at low tide had to be prepared, using gear designed and purpose-built by the R.E.'s. Two prefabricated harbours were designed and built. The floating elements they comprised were towed across the Channel by over 140 tugs. Forty thousand hospital beds were to be set up, some of which needed to be operational by D-Day.

A series of refrigerated containers to distribute blood for transfusions was put in place. Aircraft were ear-marked for rapid delivery of mail.

Schemes for a network of oil and water supply were developed. An overall plan of roads and streets was established and units each received roadmaps giving specific routes to avoid traffic jams. Where streets were too narrow, they were enlarged or bypassed.

We could continue for hours on the long list of tasks to be accomplished.
D-Day + 28: The millionth man landed.
D-Day + 38: A million tonnes of goods and 300,000 vehicles had arrived.
D-Day + 84: Late August, 2 million men had landed in Normandy, 400,000 vehicles and 3 million tonnes of goods had been unloaded.

Concurrently: 2 prefabricated ports had been built, and 55 airfields laid out, the roads from Cherbourg to Caen and from Bayeux to Tilly had been widened. Some 1,000 Bailey bridges had been erected. A ring-road south of Caen, crossing the Orne at the Athis farm was envisaged but not executed until 50 years later.

Let's not forget air traffic across the Channel and between the Normandy airfields. The flights amounted to tens of thousands and flight paths were to be scrupulously adhered to, even during round the clock attacks on the enemy, like the one on the afternoon of the 7th of August when Typhoons destroyed 300 German tanks at Mortain. Several hundred mobile radar units monitored Normandy's air space for friend and foe alike.

To all these logistic systems, the custody of POW's and the care of civilians and displaced persons was an additional task for the Allies.

About forty men were needed to assemble a Bailey Bridge; no mechanical gear was necessary. 'Quite the best thing in that line we have ever had', was Montgomery's comment. It was a certain Donald Coleman Bailey from the British Ministry of Supply who, in 1940, developed the prefabricated bridge that bears his name. Bailey Bridges are rather like a Meccano set with identical parts (1.52m x 3.05m) – 5 feet high by 10 feet long, easy to assemble by just a few men.

A Bailey Bridge in course of construction near Bénouville on the canal from Caen to the sea.

Each part consists of welded angle irons that are bolted together to form a cantilever girder. These may be in parallel series of two or three relative to the weight carried. There were standard bridges of 57 metres for loads of 40 tonnes and 45 metres for 70 tonne loads. Since parts could always be added, the bridges were very versatile and could be put in use in anything between 14 to 34 hours. The bridges across the mouth of the Orne were 100 metres long. A few weeks later, bridges of 140 to 250 metres enabled the British to cross the Seine. Over 1,000 Bailey Bridges were used in Normandy by the Allies. Practically all have now disappeared.

Bailey or Panel or even Truss Bridges (truss = cantilever or treillis) are still used in the American, British and Canadian Forces. They are often used in the event of natural catastrophes. They are also a subject of competition between military engineer units.

Churchill Bridge in Caen across the Orne.

The Cambridge dictionary defines the motor scooter as: a very light motorcycle with small wheels.

From 1936 onwards Cushman, an American, designed vehicles that corresponded to this definition and also tricycles with small wheels for the delivery of parcels, milk or even Coca-Cola. After the USA entered the war, scooters were ordered from Cushman which, though rarely seen in Normandy, were sent to Provence in August 1944 along

A Cushman parascooter.

with US Airborne Troops. The 'parascooter', recognisable thanks to its wide Harley-Davidson type leather saddle, later served as a liaison vehicle on U.S. Army airfields in France and Italy.

In Italy, Enrico Piaggio was greatly attracted by this new type of cycle. He was the son of Rinaldo Piaggio who built vehicles of all sorts, from aeroplanes to cars. It is worth noting that, on the 22nd of October 1939, the pilot Merlo Pezzi, aboard his Caproni 161 with a Rinaldo Piaggio XI 1.640 hp engine, inspired by a Gnome and Rhône model, beat the world record at an altitude of 17,083 metres, a record never surpassed by a piston-driven engine.

After the war, Enrico Piaggio, whose aircraft factory had been totally destroyed, attempted to pick up the pieces. Cushman's scooter had doubtless given him ideas.

With what remained in his ruined factories, notably small aeroplane wheels, he produced a cheap and effective means of transport, equally useful for work or pleasure to suit a large market in an Italy at the time both devastated and poor.

At noon on the 23rd of April 1946, the Vespa was patented in Florence. A year later, Ferdinando Innocenti, who was competing in the same market as Enrico Piaggio, produced a similar cycle which he patented as the Lambretta.

It is difficult to imagine, today, what life would be like for so many European teenagers, without the legendary scooter – a genuine social phenomenon.

It was surely the most audacious technological adventure ever, but also the most controversial feature of the Landings. Was it useful? Historians agree to disagree; however, the Mulberry worked and its vestiges can still be seen off Arromanches. Although the idea of bringing their port with them was first mooted in 1941 and the first study initiated in 1942, it was not until August 1943 that the concept was finalised in the course of the Quebec Conference. During Churchill and Mountbatten's

Views of the artificial harbour in Arromanches.

journey to Canada aboard the Queen Mary, a Mae West life jacket was thrown into a bath to demonstrate the effect of a floating breakwater. Mountbatten brought his staff officers into the bathroom for a demonstration. In the bath, he placed a fleet of ships made of newspaper, which sank when the water was stirred up. He repeated the experiment with his small fleet surrounded by the life jacket. The ships, protected from the swell, remained afloat. The concept of the prefabricated port, as a harbour safe for shipping, had been proved valid.

The latter months of 1943 saw intense activity, working out the details of this ambitious project. The headquarters of the Engineer in Chief were in Kingswood School near Bath. His office was a room in the school, known as the Governors' Room, with an outdoor view over an old mulberry tree, hence the codename given to the prefabricated port. The challenging undertaking was as follows:
- There were to be two ports, one for the American sector to process 5,000 tonnes daily, the other for the British sector to process 7,000 tonnes of shipping daily.
- The 150 steel or reinforced concrete parts were to be towed across the Channel.
- Each port was to take 10 Liberty Ships at a time, and the whole project was to be operational within two weeks of D-Day.
- On the 3rd of September 1943, it was decided that each port should cover an area of 600 hectares.

It was a gigantic task. Especially so for the British economy, for the nation had already borne the weight of three years at war.

Where could they possibly find the welders, riveters, joiners and the millions of tonnes of steel and reinforced concrete, or the dry docks – already occupied by ships in for refitting – and where would they find all the necessary tugs?

Work only started in December 1943. Only six months remained to recruit 30,000 men and women, the latter benefiting from a reduced working week of 54 instead of 62 hours, and no work on Sundays. The first platform was launched on the 26th of January 1944.

The completed system: floating roadways, pontoons, quays that moved up and down in time with the tide, breakwaters, special anchors, etc., were all ready by late May 1944. It took 50,000 tonnes of steel and 600,000 tonnes of reinforced concrete, amounting to a 3 million gross tonnage, to transport the complete system across the Channel the day after the 6th of June. The challenge had been met. From the 15th of June onwards, the first elements were in place. The storm that struck on the 19th of June totally destroyed the American port, and only Arromanches operated normally.

Built to take 7,000 tons of shipping daily, rising sometimes to 12,000, the daily average was 6,765 tonnes. Port Winston, as it was called, dealt with 2.5 million men, 500,000 vehicles and a million tonnes of goods.

So, useful or not? A prestigious, yet rather crazy venture? Would beach landings have sufficed? These questions remain. It can be said, however, that the techniques learnt with floating quays have been used for offshore platforms still in use today.

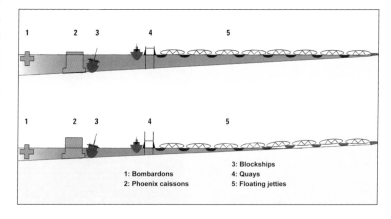

1: Bombardons
2: Phoenix caissons
3: Blockships
4: Quays
5: Floating jetties

The first known air turbine was made in Alexandria 150 years before our era. It consisted of a large vertical tube which, by the draught it created, spun a propeller on which pictures from mythology revolved.

It was only with the development of aviation, over a century ago, that any genuine interest was paid to air turbines or exhaust fumes as a supercharge for engines. Rather than in a race for performance, it was the lack of air at high altitude that led to the development of the compressor during the First World War. It was a Frenchman, Auguste Rateau, who, in 1916, suggested the fitting of compressors as a supercharge. Two methods were used: to combine

J.E. Johnson with his Spitfire IX with a turbocharger.

the compressor with the engine or to use the exhaust fumes passed through a turbine. The first method of coupling the compressor to the engine was soon abandoned since, at a certain altitude, the power used by the compressor was greater than the power it produced. The second method, that of the turbocharger – using energy from the exhaust – provided greater force.

Of all the aircraft fitted with a supercharge of this nature, two are worthy of note. They were engaged in a dogfight at 44,000 feet, a record altitude. One was a Junkers 86, fitted with a German heavy oil two-stroke diesel engine and a compressor attached, piloted by Horst Götz (who later flew the Arado 234). He was intercepted over Christchurch on his way to bomb Cardiff. His adversary, in a Spitfire with a Rolls-Royce carburettor engine fitted with a compressor, was an RAF Ace: Prince Emmanuel Galitzine, a descendant of Catherine the Great of Russia. They met at 44,000 feet in the first dogfight ever at such an altitude, in an atmosphere with little air for engines, but especially for men.

The engagement lasted 45 minutes, neither pilot gaining advantage. Horst Gödtz returned to Caen-Carpiquet exhausted. It was an unrivalled engagement in Second World War aviation. Then Mario Pezzi's feat in 1939 demonstrated that high altitudes were accessible to both men and machines.

It may be noted in passing that diesel aviation motors of the time were more powerful in relation to their weight than those fuelled by petrol. This may explain why there is renewed interest today in diesel motors for light aircraft.

211D Jumo turbocharged engine, used in particular on Junkers Ju 88 planes.

The turbocharger is now used on many vehicles and recycles exhaust fumes. It was first introduced by Saab for lorries in 1967, though it was Renault who won the French Grand Prix in 1979 with a Formula One car driven by Jabouille, that put the turbocharger in vogue for cars.

Originally a merely academic consideration, the study of natural phenomena by Aristotle, 350 years before our own era, was summed up in his work, *Meteorology*.

It provided the starting point for what only became a true science circa the 17th century, with the invention of means of measuring such phenomena: the thermometer by Galileo and the barometer by Torricelli. In 1892, by launching a balloon carrying a thermometer and a barometer, two Frenchmen – G. Hermite and G. Besançon – made a major step towards weather forecasting.

Two members of the W.A.A.E with a Theodolite about to take the bearings of a weather balloon.

It was with information gathered at sea, just after the First World War, that aircraft obtained the data needed to cross the Atlantic.

In the Second World War, shipping and aviation pooled their resources. In fact, mastery of the seas involved knowledge of atmospheric conditions. The weather, which could prove to be friend or foe, was increasingly better understood as the conflict continued. It could be said, for example, that the weather befriended the Allies during the evacuation of the British Expeditionary Force from Dunkirk in June 1940 with a clear sky and calm sea, to become their enemy, but a friend to the Germans, in June 1944.

Between the two dates however, great progress in weather forecasting had been made. In 1940, there were four daily flights to determine weather conditions for the Air Ministry. In 1944, there

were thirty, some at an altitude of 44,000 feet. Use was also made of balloons and smoke shells, and of course radar to locate cloud formations. In 1942, the struggle to obtain command of the seas went hand in hand with assaults on weather stations. Often camouflaged as fishing vessels, they could disseminate details on weather gathered by ships. Up to that time, radio silence was of the essence for shipping, to avoid giving away their position to U-boats. Morse by lamp was widely used, even in home ports.

Hence, on the eve of the Landings, a five-day weather forecast was attempted. The weather, as we now all know, was deplorably uncertain in early June 1944. Consequently, on the morning of the 4th of June, Operation Overlord was postponed. The Germans themselves considered any invasion at that time impossible.

Eisenhower declared on that same Sunday morning, 4th June, that the weather conditions were such that Allied air supremacy could not be guaranteed, and given that it was the key to success, the landings in Normandy must be postponed.

On the evening of the 4th, at 21:00 hours, Group Captain J.M. Stagg, in charge of weather reports, forecast a lull on Tuesday 6th, though the final decision could not be taken until a later forecast had been made at 04:30 on the 5th, confirming the previous day's estimations. The rest is history, and Air Ministry forecasts, along with other armed services, had just earned itself a reputation. It may also be noted to what extent weather forecasting has proved to be a determining factor in the course of history. On the 4th of August 1944, a column of 400 German tanks from six different divisions advanced towards Mortain (on orders issued by Hitler on the 2nd). The aim was to cut off Patton's tanks from his base. The forecast was favourable; low cloud gave cover from air attacks and success was assured. The forecast however allowed for possible cloud breaks around midday and British 'tank buster' Typhoons were on the ready.

At 12:30, they began a 'round the clock' attack that destroyed half the enemy's tanks. Smoke from the burning vehicles, however, was so intense that the attack was called off for nearly two hours, before continuing till evening. This was the first time that aircraft had played a determining role in a land-based battle. Today, satellites involved in very sophisticated computer programmes offer considerable developments in weather forecasting.

Aerosols

Research on the use of gases in warfare – bacteriological or otherwise – led to the development of moisture sprays containing chemical or biological micro-particles. It was a Frenchman specialising in ultrafiltration who invented aerolisation before the last war. In 1941, he brought his plans and formula for aerosol bombs to the attention of the Allies.

The Americans produced an insecticide aerosol can, using a DDT base, filled first with carbon dioxide and later with Freon. It was used by them in the Philippines against the Anopheles mosquito. During the Landings, all the Allied formations used aerosol insecticides in addition to powder. One aerosol can could disinfect 28 cubic metres.

Finally, regarding Japan, the Americans hesitated between the use of the atomic bomb and aerosol defoliants, sprayed from the air to destroy rice crops; the resulting famine would supposedly have induced surrender. As with DDT, Freon which is a threat to the ozone layer was taken out of use.

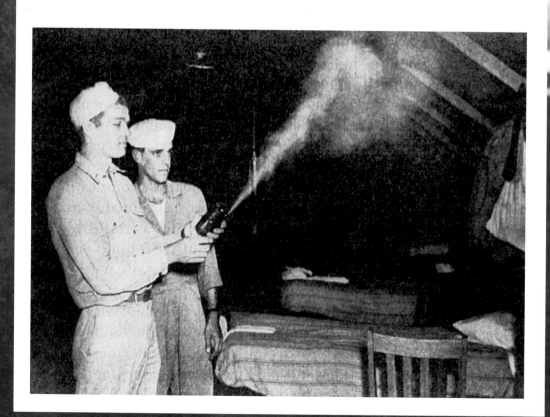

Ray-Ban

After crossing the Atlantic with a balloon in 1921, (6 years before Lindberg's transatlantic flight), Lt John Macready of the U.S. Army Air Force suffered from headaches and nausea caused by the strong sunlight at high altitudes.

A few years later, the U.S. Forces invited firms to bring out protective sunglasses with panoramic vision. It was a protective measure for their pilots and an aid to spotting enemy planes in dive attacks under the sun.

Bausch & Lomb suggested a green tinted lens with an ultraviolet and infrared filter and, in 1936, marketed an anti-reflective lens that absorbed and reflected part of the solar spectrum, as per USAAF specifications. On the 7th of May 1937, Bausch & Lomb patented the name 'Ray-Ban' (their product 'banished' discomforting 'rays', hence the name Ray-Ban), those famous 'large metal' framed glasses we are all so familiar with today.

General Mark Clark and General Eisenhower wearing Ray-Ban sunglasses in 1943.

They were 'official issue' in the U.S. Air Force, but were widely used by all GIs. Ray-Ban glasses landed on the Normandy coast in 1944, later to become — just like the Zippo, the t-shirt, jeans and many more… legendary and timeless accessories.

IN DAILY USE

The Zippo

The Zippo storm lighter is 'the only lighter that never fails to light,' according to Eisenhower. It was on sale in all the PX stores (U.S. equivalent of NAAFI) and landed in Normandy with the U.S. troops. Along with Ray-Ban sunglasses, it was destined to become a legend.

In 1933, G.G. Blaisdell put together a lighter, based on a 19th century model available in the Austrian Army, for which he obtained a patent in 1934.

During the war, he developed two types of lighter. Up to 1943, the metallic lighter in polished steel with an internal hinge in four sections was the only one on sale. It was succeeded by the Black Crackle Finish for reasons of economy, and had a hinge of only three sections and was on sale to U.S. Forces only. The black crackle finish paint, covering some base metal became a vehicle of expression akin to First World War trench art. On the black paint, the GIs scratched all their fantasies, achievements or merely a place or an event. The oldest or most elaborately decorated are particularly appreciated by collectors and considered of great value, especially as they carry a life guarantee, the manufacturer having undertaken to repair them free of charge.

ZIPPO
(1933 - 1954)

ZIPPO
(1955 - 1979)

Zippo
(1980 - 2011)

Ball-point pen

Although a patent had been taken out in 1888 by an American, J.J. Laud, for a large marker suitable for use on parcels, it was a Hungarian, Laszlo Biró, who invented the ball-point pen in 1938. He had noticed that when children's marbles landed in a puddle, they left a mark on the ground. Biró patented his pen in Hungary before leaving for Argentine to escape the Nazis. There, he produced his pens under the trade mark: Birome. Just prior to the war, he conceded the patent rights to Eversharp and its associate, the ink manufacturer Faber. Reynolds also produced its own ball-point pen.

In 1943-44, having heard that this type of pen did not leak at high altitude, the RAF asked the United States to supply them with a pen of such magical qualities for its bomber air crews, exasperated by pens that leaked at varying altitudes and the indelible pencils of the time that left blue marks on the tongue. Quite often, during annual commemorations of the Landings, tales of leaking pens and of the welcome advent of the Biro are still repeated today. Some veterans remember that, back at base, the Biro enabled them to write, even in the rain.

The pen, however, was not problem-free: not quite spherical, excessively or insufficiently fluid ink, no ink level indicator, etc. Consumer complaints led Eversharp Reynolds and Douglas to concede the American market to Parker.

In France, Baron Bich's tiny Compagnie de Moulages, established in Clichy, also made pens; they approached Biro, obtained rights and put in a patent for a 'Carcasse pour un appareil scripteur' (shell for a writing device) in 1951 and, in 1952, produced the Bic Cristal pen. Striking success followed, due notably to an ambitious international policy. They took over Biro-Swan in England, and more recently Sheaffer, selling millions of Bic pens worldwide – a genuine success story – French style.

The T-shirt

The T-type shirt or Training-shirt was a standard issue vest in the U.S. Navy and the result of submissions by clothing firms in 1942. Contrary to what its name implies it was in fact an undergarment worn for fatigues.

Both Hanes and Union Underwear, two firms supplying the U.S. Navy, claim to have stocked it before 1942.

The presence of American ships in all corners of the globe assured the T-shirt with lightning success. Like many other garments, such as jeans, it became a tradition and a basic garment for several generations. The T-shirt has now become a genuine means of communication, its wearer becoming akin to a sandwich man.

Baseball players,
U.S. Navy.

THE AUTHOR

Philippe Bauduin was fourteen when he first met the Royal Engineers on the Normandy battlefields. He served as a photo interpreter officer in the 2/33 Squadron of the French Air Force before beginning a civil career in 1958 as a research engineer in solid state physics, optics and microwaves. In 1974, he was in charge of the Great National Heavy Ion Accelerator project in Caen. In 1980, he joined the French National Agency for Research Development (ANVAR), where he led the Innovation Engineering and Technology Transfer Department. Now retired, he lives in his country cottage, an ex-Royal Engineer pump house, where he spends a large share of his time preserving the name of the Royal Engineers and writing about their works in Normandy.

Philippe Bauduin, who has also published papers on airfield construction, and has been awarded the Legion d'Honneur.

ACKNOWLEDGMENTS

To all those who have assisted whether orally or in writing with their recollections, documents, articles and objects, and who offered their encouragement:

Dr. J.-P. Bénamou, M. Brissard, E. Chaunu, Colonel G. Legout, D. Mary (who sadly, will not have the chance to see this in print), Dr. J.-P. Rioult, F. Robinard, General Scott-Bowden, J.-M. Selles and E. Allain, E. Sommer, T. B. & M .M. Greenhalgh Firms: Bic, Bausch & Lomb (Ray-Ban), Motorola, Thomson-CSF, and especially to Admiral C. Brac de La Perrière.

S. Lajoye and S. Youf, Éditions OREP.

Photographic credits:

P. Bauduin, CAEN - DITE USIS, PARIS - C. Prime - Nobel Foundation, STOCKHOLM - Imperial War Museum, LONDON - King's College, CAMBRIDGE - Musée de l'Air et de l'Espace, LE BOURGET - Musée Mémorial de la Bataille de Normandie, BAYEUX - Musée D-Day Omaha, VIERVILLE - National Archives, WASHINGTON - Public Record Office, KEw - Submarine Museum, GOSPORT.

OREP
EDITIONS

Zone tertiaire de Nonant - 14400 BAYEUX
Tel.: (33) 02 31 51 81 31 – Fax: 02 31 51 81 32
Email: info@orepeditions.com - Website: www.orepeditions.com

Editor: Grégory Pique
Editorial coordination: Sophie Lajoye
Graphic design - Layout: Sophie Youf

ISBN : 978-2-8151-0539-2 – © Éditions OREP 2020
Legal deposit: 2nd quarter 2020